CRYSTAL
Connections

CRYSTAL
Connections

understand the messages of 101 essential crystals
and how to connect with their wisdom

PHILIP PERMUTT

From the best-selling author of
The Crystal Healer: Volume 1
and *Volume 2*

CICO BOOKS
LONDON NEW YORK

Published in 2023 by CICO Books
An imprint of Ryland Peters & Small Ltd
20–21 Jockey's Fields   341 E 116th St
London WC1R 4BW   New York, NY 10029

www.rylandpeters.com

10 9 8 7 6 5 4 3 2 1

Text © Philip Permutt 2023
Design, illustration, and photography
© CICO Books 2023

See page 144 for further picture credits

A CIP catalog record for this book is available from the Library of Congress and the British Library.

ISBN: 978-1-80065-209-5

Printed in China

Senior commissioning editor: Carmel Edmonds
Editor: Slav Todorov
Senior designer: Emily Breen
Photographers: Roy Palmer & Geoff Dann
Illustrator: Trina Dalziel
Art director: Sally Powell
Creative director: Leslie Harrington
Production manager:
Gordana Simakovic
Publishing manager: Penny Craig

FSC® MIX Paper | Supporting responsible forestry FSC® C008047

SAFETY NOTE

Please note that while the descriptions of the properties of crystals refer to healing benefits, they are not intended to replace diagnosis of illness or ailments, or healing or medicine. Always consult your doctor or other health professional in the case of illness.

Contents

Introduction 6

Chapter One
STONE PEOPLE 8

Crystals are Living Beings 10

Crystal Energy 14

Tuning in to Living Crystals 22

Crystal Colors 27

Chapter Two
YOUR CRYSTAL FRIENDS 32

Am I Crazy to Talk to My Crystals? 34

Cleansing Crystals 39

Do You Choose Crystals—
Or Do They Choose You? 44

What Makes Some Crystals
Special to Me? 47

Chapter Three
WORKING WITH CRYSTALS 52

Where Are Crystals Found? 54

Welcoming New Crystals
into Your Home 60

How to Work with Crystals 63

Chapter Four
THE HUMAN
ENERGY SYSTEM 72

What Is the Human Energy System? 74

Chakras and Meridians 77

Chapter Five
CRYSTAL DIVINATION 90

What is Divination? 92

Chapter Six
THE CRYSTAL FINDER 102

Crystal Index 140

General Index 142

Acknowledgments 144

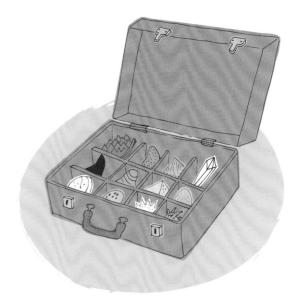

Introduction:
When the Stone People Spoke to Me

It was the year 1991…I had suffered from Crohn's disease for a decade and had had a couple of bowel re-sections. That's when a surgeon removes part of your gut and then sticks the rest back together with a giant staple gun! This year it was different. I had another bowel re-section, but this time the sciatic nerve going to my right leg was stuck to my small bowel in multiple places, causing excruciating and continuous pain. The surgeons didn't think they could separate the nerve from the bowel cleanly. The options were:

(1) hopefully, but very unlikely, the nerve and bowel could be separated;

(2) remove the bowel: side-effect, colostomy bag for the rest of my life; or

(3) sever the sciatic nerve to stop the pain—the side effect of this being that I wouldn't be able to walk again.

At the age of 31, this is a hell of a decision to have to make.

Anyway, following the operation the doctor said, "The operation was a great success, but I'm sorry, you can't walk." And this was the moment in time that I suddenly became interested in alternative therapies!

Over the next few weeks, I tried many different energy therapies, including a lot of crystal healing. One day, I wanted to have a cigarette (yes, back then, like so many other people, I smoked). You were allowed to smoke in one place inside the hospital (yes, back then, you were allowed to smoke in hospitals!). This area was in a corridor by an open window. I was in a room off the corridor, in a bed, with lots of tubes running into me, and I couldn't walk. I had this drip going into my left arm and that was on a wheelie stand. On the other side of the bed was a big contraption pumping pre-digested food into my heart. Fascinating…I always wondered who digested the food for me! Anyway, I recall somehow managing to maneuver the two wheeled stands to the edge of the bed, into the corridor, and toward the open window in the corridor. And finally, there I was, peacefully minding my own business and

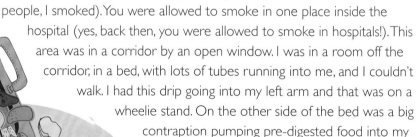

having a quiet smoke when a nurse appeared and said: "What are you doing here?" And I thought to myself, here we go, the smoking lecture. Then she said, "You can't walk, get back to bed!" And that was the moment of realization that, firstly, I could walk again and, secondly, these weird energy treatments I'd been having really worked!

With the aid of my two now-trusted wheeled contraptions, I "walked" back to my room. The first thing I saw was a quartz crystal next to my bed and he said, "So, now you get it." That was the first time I ever heard a crystal speak. I didn't imagine it; I felt it through my being. Wow!

Six weeks and two days later, I walked out of the hospital, albeit slowly, without the aid of crutches or walking sticks.

The next 12 months were spent convalescing, acquiring crystals, and learning to listen to their messages. Over the next 30 years, I learned about the amazing Stone People, listening to them and learning their language, healing myself and healing others, and teaching crystal healing and writing books about it.

Crystal Connections sets out to show you my methods for tapping into and understanding these amazing Stone People and the messages they bring us. In my opinion, if crystals can talk, then they must be living…let's connect with them.

Chapter One
STONE PEOPLE

Are crystals alive? Well, we're going to delve into the concept of crystals as living beings and how they might be the original source of DNA and complex life as we know it.

Then we'll explore crystal energy and some of the ways it affects us. You will discover practical exercises to show you how you can tune in to crystal energy and listen to the messages your crystals hold for you.

Crystals Are Living Beings

Many moons ago, I did a degree in Applied Biology. The question always asked during my studies was what is the borderline of life? In other words, what is the lowest evolutionary level at which something can be described as alive? Biologists agree that for an organism to be considered as living, then it or its species must be able to eat, grow, and reproduce. About half of all biologists will tell you that the lowest organism on the evolutionary scale is a bacterium, which is a single-celled organism that has a cell wall but no central nucleus, whereas the other half say it is a virus, a core of RNA or DNA genetic material surrounded by a protective coat of protein.

So, let's explore the difference between bacteria and viruses. Imagine an experiment in which you take some bacteria and put them in a petri dish. This is a plastic dish, often used in laboratories, with a tight-fitting cover and half-filled with a growth medium, which is a liquid or gel that contains everything the bacteria need to survive. If you leave the dish in the corner of a lab, when you come back the following week, there will be lots and lots of bacteria because they have eaten the growth medium, grown slightly, and reproduced massively.

Bacteria

You cannot do this with viruses because they are only able to replicate inside the living cells of a specific host. In fact, viruses are highly specialized and must be in a very specific host environment in order to thrive. However, if you kept them in the specific environment for that species of virus, then you would find they had eaten their environment, grown a little, and reproduced a lot.

The only difference between bacteria and viruses is that the latter need to be in their own specific growing medium. In general, a virus that affects your lungs cannot infect those of your cat; the virus that makes your budgie's feathers fall out cannot affect you; and the virus that infects your skin cannot infect your kidneys—viruses are usually that specific. Interestingly, this is also why on the very rare occasion that a virus jumps species, we have a pandemic, just like the one caused by the coronavirus SARS-CoV-2.

Virus

Coronavirus SARS-CoV-2

ARE CRYSTALS ALIVE TOO?

Now let's explore whether crystals are also living organisms, using the definitions used by biologists for all life forms—that they can eat, grow, and reproduce:

Crystals can eat Crystals eat the environment in which they are growing, as this contains readily available building blocks of the mineral from which they are made. Quartz crystals, for example, "eat" oxygen and silicon from their surroundings, while selenite requires oxygen, hydrogen, calcium, and sulfur to grow.

Crystals can grow Crystals grow , which is why you find small ones and large ones! The larger ones were once little crystals too.

Crystals can reproduce Crystals reproduce in two ways: through separation and seeding. Separation occurs if a crystal breaks away from its crystal family while it is growing, which can be caused by earthquakes, the Earth's tectonic movements, or even lightning strikes. When this happens, the crystal sometimes starts to produce "babies" at the broken end. These are often called self-healed crystals.

In seeding, small pieces of crystal break off and act as a "seed" for a new crystal. Dust particles in the growing medium can also act as a seed to start the crystal-growing process (see Cairns-Smith, A. G., *Seven Clues to the Origin of Life*, CUP, 1985). To understand the seeding reproduction method, we must consider the age of a crystal and the age of the planet, and recognize that we as human beings cannot begin to comprehend these huge expanses of time. Crystals exist on a different time scale to us, with many being millions, hundreds of millions, or even billions of years old. For example, although quartz and selenite crystals can be ancient, some are still growing and even the younger ones may have started growing when dinosaurs roamed the Earth, and the youngest may have been seeded today. The oldest crystals, such as zircon, formed when the

Self-healed crystal

Earth first became solid around four billion years ago.

If you destroy a quartz crystal, smashing it into a million pieces and scattering them, each small piece of crystal that ends up in the perfect growing environment for quartz crystals will act as a seed crystal and grow into a new crystal. Quartz crystals are found all over the world because over the last four billion years every part of the Earth's surface has, at one time or another, provided the perfect growing environment for quartz crystals. Then, over the next 11 billion years—before we disappear into the Sun—it is likely that every area of the planet's surface will, at different times, continue to provide the perfect growing environment for quartz.

Therefore, we can perhaps class crystals as living beings because, just like viruses, they need a specific growing environment in which to flourish. If we regard viruses as living, then surely the same applies to crystals?

Zircon

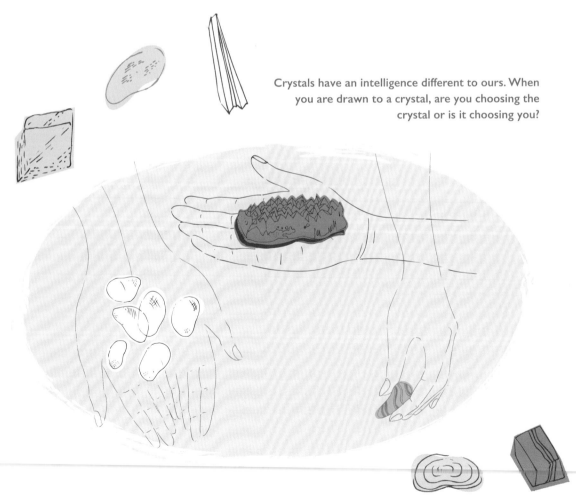

Crystals have an intelligence different to ours. When you are drawn to a crystal, are you choosing the crystal or is it choosing you?

SACRED PIPESTONE

Fascinatingly, the sacred pipestone, which is used to make the ceremonial pipes of America's First Nation peoples, is catlinite (or kaolinite), one of the very crystals purported to be the first form of life.

Catlinite rough rock

THE SOURCE OF LIFE?

Crystals are likely to be the source of life on Earth, possibly creating the genetic code of life—the RNA/DNA polymers containing the genetic instructions that allow complex organisms to replicate (see Cairns-Smith, A. G. and H. Hartman (eds), *Clay Minerals and the Origin of Life*, CUP, 1987). In fact, some scientists believe crystals could even be our oldest ancestors (see Cairns-Smith, A. G., Oliver and Boyd, *The Life Puzzle*, University of Toronto Press, 1971)! Although this may seem improbable, I like to remember the following lines from Arthur Conan Doyle's *The Adventures of Sherlock Holmes*: "It is an old maxim of mine that when you exclude the impossible, whatever remains, however improbable, must be the truth."

Catlinite

Crystal Energy

Crystals are all around us every day. Most people think of crystals as the pretty items you can buy in crystal stores and gift stores, but I like to include the whole mineral kingdom in my colloquial use of the word "crystal." So, this includes crystals, gems, jewelry gemstones, rocks, pebbles on the beach or in your backyard, sacred monoliths and stone circles, and even a mountain made of crystals, rocks, and minerals. Just as individual crystals can "talk" to you, so the land speaks to you too. You will also find crystals inside today's modern gadgets and technology, such as quartz and tourmaline crystals with their solid state electric field in electrical circuits and rubies in laser technology. In fact, our entire 21st-century lifestyle is based on crystal technology.

Ruby in laser
technology

The Cradle of Humankind lies about 50km (31 miles) northwest of Johannesburg, in the Republic of South Africa. Declared a World Heritage Site by UNESCO in 1999,

Cradle of Humankind, Republic of South Africa

the area is home to the world's largest number of fossils of our human ancestors. There is a series of caves in the region that contain the earliest human remains found so far. These include some species of hominid, primates (including humans), and their ancient, bipedal, upright-walking relatives who evolved into you and me, as well as several that disappeared along the evolutionary ladder. They were found at different levels in the caves as archeologists excavated the sites over many years. Connecting all these different species is the use of crystals in the form of stone tools, which have been found at every level of the caves. This means that around 3.3 million years ago, our ancestors invented a primitive form of crystal technology—and we're still using crystals in technology today.

Ancient human remains

CONNECTING WITH CRYSTAL ENERGY

In this book, I am more interested in the subtle energies of crystals, as it is these that influence people. You may have noticed this when you go into a crystal store or visit a friend with an abundance of crystals in their home. The place just feels different, and it is this sense of difference that we are going to explore.

To help you feel and experience crystal energy for yourself, using each of your five senses—hearing, sight, smell, taste, and touch—I'm going to show you a practical meditation exercise. Some people talk about also having a special sense, although I'm not sure we need this at all because our five natural senses are enough for us to connect with crystals. However, we do need to stretch our five senses as much as we can to sense subtle energies. Everyone can do this, although some people find it easier and are sometimes described as having a sixth sense. But this is essentially just one or more of their five well-trained senses. So, you don't need an extra-special sixth sense to connect with crystals, but simply to turn your "ordinary" five senses into extraordinary ones.

exercise: SENSING CRYSTAL ENERGY

You can do this exercise with any type of crystal, but I find a natural quartz crystal is the easiest to start with. Once you have a little experience, try the exercise with each crystal in your collection. Rest assured that the size of your collection doesn't matter—as soon as you have two crystals, you have a collection!

Sometimes it can be helpful to play some relaxing music during this exercise (and the many others throughout the book). It enables you to get "into the zone," focus your senses, and hide any small, distracting noises around you. I always play my album *Walking the Walk* for this, but you can listen to anything that helps you relax and focus.

Blue Mist Lemurian quartz

1 **Prepare** Treat the exercise like a meditation and do the Meditation Preparation (see box, page 18) before you start.
2 **See the crystal** Hold a quartz crystal in your hand and look at it. Examine the crystal closely with your eyes. Take your time with this and allow yourself to notice all the details of the crystal's surface: the flat parts, the uneven areas, and any shapes or patterns that catch your eye. Make sure you do this for each of the six sides, the termination, and the base of the crystal.
3 **Feel the crystal** Now close your eyes and repeat the process with your fingertips, exploring the crystal with your sense of touch. Feel the smooth elements and the rough sections, the pointy bits, the sharp edges and point, and the regions that feel hard or soft in your hand. It's strange, but when you're sensing energy, some areas of a solid rock can feel "soft."
4 **Hear the crystal** Next, hold one of the sides of the crystal close to your ear (about 5–10mm/¼–½in. away) and listen. As you listen, you will start to notice a gentle sound emanating from the crystal, which is its physical vibration. Many people say this is like the sound you hear when you hold a seashell to your ear, but not quite the same. This is because of how the sound is generated. With a seashell the air flows into the closed

spiral of the shell and you hear it rushing out again, whereas with a crystal you are listening to the physical vibration of the crystal. If you have difficulty hearing this crystal vibration, try holding different sides of the crystal, or one end or the other, close to your ear. In the same way that you can see and touch the crystal, you can also quite naturally hear the crystal vibrations.

5 **Smell the crystal** Then go through the same process with your nose, holding the crystal under your nose and sniffing it. Yes, crystals have an individual smell.

6 **Taste the crystal** First make sure the crystal is physically clean, washing it thoroughly in dishwashing liquid—the better brands are gentler on crystals as well as your hands—and rinsing it under running water from the tap, or a bottle or stream if you prefer (see page 40). Then place the crystal on the end of your tongue, so you can taste it. You'll find that each type of crystal has a different taste.

7 **Keep practicing** As you explore your crystal collection, you will notice more and more subtle differences between how your crystal friends look, feel, sound, smell, and taste. This exercise will also increase the range of your senses and you will become more aware of energies and sensations in your everyday world.

Safety Note: Please do not perform the last part of this exercise—the tasting—with any crystal that has a "No Elixir" warning in the Crystal Finder (see pages 102–39). For more on washing and cleansing crystals, and why this should be avoided in some cases, see page 39. Please also note that some crystals, such as selenite and celestite, may be damaged by water, so omit the tasting part of this exercise if you cannot safely wash your crystal.

MEDITATION PREPARATION

You should do this preparation before all the meditations in the book. Find a quiet, comfortable place where you will not be disturbed. If you live with other people, ask not to be disturbed or perhaps put a "Do Not Disturb" sign on your door. If you have children or pets, make sure they are occupied and won't need anything from you for a while. Unplug your telephone and turn off your cell phone. Wear comfortable clothes; if you are wearing anything tight-fitting like a belt or tie, take it off or loosen it, so you are not restricted. Make yourself comfortable and sit upright, with your feet on the floor or your legs crossed. Take three slow, deep breaths, breathing in through your nose and out through your mouth. In your mind, imagine tree roots growing from your feet into the earth beneath you. See them go deeper and deeper into the earth, grounding you before you begin to meditate.

CRYSTAL ENERGY—WITH A LITTLE HELP FROM MY FRIENDS

Once you realize that you can sense crystal energy, it becomes very easy to apply crystals to most situations in your everyday life—if you're feeling sad or low, for example, or when a little inspiration would help you. You start to sense when you need a specific crystal and hear when one is calling you. You begin listening to your crystal friends. And, yes, they do become friends! Like human friends, some crystals will come and go in your life, while others will become lifelong companions. As a result, I always avoid the word "use" in my crystal books because I really do treat all my crystals as friends—you wouldn't "use" a friend, would you? I work with crystals, carry and hold them, talk to them, and listen to them. Sometimes I play with them, and I always listen to their wisdom. Remember, crystals have been around for millions and sometimes billions of years, so they potentially carry a great deal of wisdom.

Calcite

Keep some tumble polished stones in each room of your home, so you always have a variety of crystals handy whenever you need them—by filling your home with crystals, you'll be filling it with love!

GETTING STARTED—HOW CRYSTALS CAN HELP

Here are some thoughts on how you can simply and easily call on crystals every day to enhance your life and help you deal with various issues. For more on this, see the Crystal Finder, pages 102–39.

Calcite

Restore tranquility Bring peace to your home with Himalayan salt lamps. These are made from halite (rock salt) and produce negative ions that will freshen a room. You can also place large calcite crystals or rocks all around the home.

Selenite

Combat negative energy Selenite lamps and crystals will help cleanse your home or office of unhelpful energies.

Quartz

Transform negativity Crystals such as amethyst and clear quartz clusters and crystal balls can absorb negativity from people and transform that energy into something positive and helpful. They can make your home feel much better after an argument.

Amethyst

Relax and unwind Amethyst brings a deep sense of relaxation and so is welcome in any space where you like to chill out, such as your living room or bedroom. Amethyst geodes are super powerful for this and bring a feeling of spirituality and spiritual love to your home. Adding rose quartz to your bath can also help you relax and promotes soft skin too.

Rose quartz

Provide protection Tourmaline crystals can create a bubble of energetic protection around your home, or anywhere or anyone you like. Carry a tourmaline crystal with you and give one to someone you love! You can also wear tourmaline crystals in pieces of jewelry or carry them in a pocket or small neck bag, or even pop one in your bra (if you wear one). Place larger ones in your home, office, or workplace and car.

Tourmaline

Be inspired Place pyrite and citrine where you work to bring sparks of inspiration and abundance to your endeavors.

Pyrite

Increase sensitivity Wear or carry lapis lazuli to make you more aware of the energies around you. With a little practice, this crystal will tell you how other people are really feeling.

Lapis lazuli

Rhodochrosite

Malachite

Sugilite

Calcite

Jasper

Increase loving energy A bedroom recipe might include rose quartz for both loving yourself and creating or reinforcing a loving relationship. Rhodochrosite brings passion to any relationship; malachite aids sleep and helps to restore broken sleep patterns.

Deal with worry If you're worrying about anything, hold tourmaline or sugilite to help ease your mind.

Calm and release Blue calcite is good for calming babies and children, while orange calcite can help you release trapped emotions and turn them into laughter.

Heal and restore Quartz crystal will help with any healing. Although there may be a better crystal for a specific issue, quartz is good for everything, whether this is a physical, mental, emotional, or spiritual problem.

Treat indoor plants Add brecciated jasper, clear quartz, and agate to your indoor plant pots to promote healthy growth.

Crazy lace agate

CRYSTAL POWER—A QUICK EXPERIMENT

If you already have a few crystals, you can try a little experiment. Move them all into one room, then observe the reaction of visitors as they go from room to room and enter the one with the crystals. This room will feel different to all the others in your home, and everyone will notice the difference, even if they don't know what it is or understand what they are are feeling.

Tuning in to Living Crystals

When I receive a new crystal, I like to get to know it. There's no right or wrong way to do this, in the same way that there's no right or wrong way to get to know a new friend or work colleague. Personally, I like to keep my new crystal nearby. If it's small enough, I'll keep it in my pocket, then take it out, hold it, feel its energy, and listen to anything that it has to say.

Each of us is drawn to certain crystals. You could be looking at a shelf of amethyst, for example, and you may like them all, but only one or maybe a few of them will speak to you. Before you hear them, you sense them. One crystal might appear brighter or more purple or have a better shape. This is because that crystal is saying: "Hey! I'm over here! Me! Me! Choose meeeee!"

Amethyst

When you find this special crystal, go for it! I've lost count of the number of times I have seen people come into my crystal showroom over the last 30 years and, almost as soon as they come in, they will pick up a crystal that's calling to them. It's as if they completely understand the crystal and know what it's saying and why. Then they put it down. So far, they have been in the showroom for one to three minutes. They will then spend the next 30 minutes to an hour looking at other crystals in the showroom. They may even ask to see some of the crystals in the storeroom too. And then, eventually, they will pick up the first crystal they saw and buy it!

So, ask yourself: when you are drawn to a crystal, are you choosing the crystal or is it choosing you? Let me give you an example from personal experience. I have a citrine crystal that I regard as my writing crystal because it is always by my side when I'm writing. But it wasn't always like that. In around 2003, I was at the Tucson Gem & Mineral Show, which takes place every year in Arizona, USA, and this crystal literally "screamed" at me across the room! It was brighter than any crystal nearby and shone with a golden citrine light that was full of rainbows. I had no idea what this citrine crystal was saying, but I understood that he had chosen me. I went straight over and picked him up, and he was so happy—full of energy and light and buzzing in my hands. A tingle went up my spine. I took him home and as soon as I unpacked him it was as if he had gone to sleep. For the next four years my crystal was moved to

different rooms, placed in and out of the sun, on a table, a bookshelf, or a window ledge, next to the bed, in the bathroom…

The author's citrine writing crystal

Then, one day in 2007, I was eating breakfast at the kitchen table, opening the mail, when I heard a crystal scream from the window ledge and saw this bright golden light full of rainbows! My crystal was trying to tell me something. I looked at the envelope I had just picked up to open…It was the contract for my first book and my citrine crystal has never been quiet since! In fact, he's here right now as I write.

CONNECTING WITH CRYSTAL FRIENDS USING A PENDULUM

One of the simplest and most effective ways of communicating with crystals is with with the help of a crystal pendulum. It is such an easy way for anyone to start listening to the Stone People. The pendulum works in the same way as dowsing, which is a natural ability that everyone possesses. Whether for finding water, searching for missing objects, or predicting the sex of a baby, we've been dowsing since time immemorial. Although some people are naturally better at dowsing than others, with a little practice anyone can easily learn how to work with a pendulum.

Dowsing comes from the idea of water divining, a practice used to locate water, usually with a dowsing rod made from a forked twig, but today you can just buy pendulums and dowsing rods instead. Although a pendulum can be made of almost anything, I prefer to work with crystal pendulums, as these are much easier to work with, especially when you begin. The crystal on a crystal pendulum gives you an instant crystal helper too—there's an interaction with the crystal as well as the pendulum!

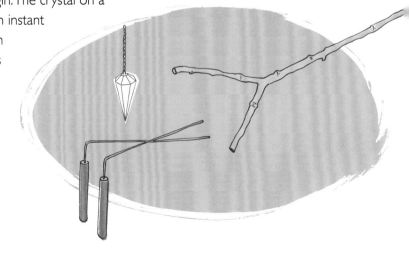

Your Inner Pendulum

We all have an inner pendulum. This is the part of us inside, somewhere near our stomach, that goes up to say "yes" and sinks down to say "no." Everyone is sometimes aware of this, but we usually only hear our inner pendulum when it is speaking to us in extreme moments. It is the feeling that rises through your body, lifts you up, and shouts "Wow! This is amazing!" when you experience something brilliant and the sinking feeling you get when your stomach seems to fall through your body to the floor and says, "Get me out of here NOW!" We've all experienced these feelings at some point in our lives, but your body is doing this all the time—your inner pendulum is working round the clock.

You experience small, subtle movements that say "yes" and "no" to everything you do, everyone you meet, everywhere you go, what you watch and listen to, and even as you are reading this. It is a natural mechanism, trying to guide you safely through life. When you work with a crystal pendulum, it is showing you an external physical manifestation of what your inner pendulum is doing inside you.

The more you work with your crystal pendulum, the more you will recognize your inner pendulum and, over time, the less you will need its help.

WORKING WITH A CRYSTAL PENDULUM

Here are a few points to bear in mind when working with a crystal pendulum:

- Pendulums are the simplest spiritual tool there is.
- Pendulums are wonderful because they only answer "yes" or "no."
- Pendulums can be frustrating because they only answer "yes" or "no."
- If you treat a pendulum as a spiritual tool, then it will always give you the correct answer. If you treat it as a game, it will treat you as a game too.

CHOOSING AND WORKING WITH A CRYSTAL PENDULUM

You can have more than one crystal pendulum for different purposes. So, when you choose a pendulum, be clear in your mind about why you want it. Is it for general questions, personal enquiries, or healing, for example, or perhaps for treating clients? I have three similar amethyst pendulums that I work with when teaching: one to work with, a backup pendulum, and one just in case. I have another pendulum made of lapis lazuli in my therapy room for working with clients and a citrine one at home to answer any personal queries.

Lapis lazuli

Let's start by choosing one pendulum. If you can, visit a crystal or metaphysical store where there's likely to be a selection to choose from. Alternatively, you can search online, as long as there's a good selection available. Let's look at both options in turn:

Choosing a Pendulum in Store

Center yourself before you go inside. Spend a minute in the parking lot or even outside the door. Take a few deep breaths, breathing in slowly through your nose and out through your mouth. Imagine your feet are like the roots of a tree. See them going deep into the ground. When you feel still, centered, and grounded, make your way into the store. Don't look at anything other than the pendulum display. If the display is not obvious, then ask—don't explore the store. Stay focused. Look at the selection of crystal pendulums and let one choose you. You might hear it call to you, or it might be brighter than all the others. Perhaps it wobbles or connects with you energetically.

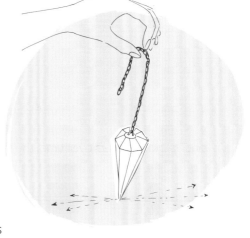

Take this pendulum. Hold the top of the chain or the bead at the top, if there is one, and ask it to show you a "yes." Be patient. The pendulum will move in one of four ways: forwards and backwards, side to side, or in a clockwise or counterclockwise circle. Don't worry if you only see a very small movement; it will get bigger as you work with the pendulum. Then ask the pendulum to show you a "no." You will see a different one of the four possible movements, so you now know what your pendulum's "yes" and "no" answers look like.

Once you have identified the "yes" and "no" answers, your first question should always be: "Are you a good pendulum for me to work with?". If it answers "yes," that's great—you have chosen your pendulum. If it answers "no," then put that pendulum back and start the whole process again with another one. The amazing thing is that if you follow the simple guidance given here, the right pendulum for you will always be the first one.

Choosing a Pendulum Online

To select your pendulum online, look for a website with a dedicated pendulum page. Open this page and you should see a good selection of pendulums. Close your eyes, take three slow, deep breaths in through your nose and slowly exhale each time through your mouth. Imagine tree roots coming out of your feet into the ground. Now, because you are online, imagine there's a cord connecting you to the computer screen, as if you've been plugged into it. In your mind, see the energy flowing in both directions and feel this electrical connection. When you feel this connection, open your eyes and be aware of the first pendulum you notice. This will be the right one.

When the pendulum is delivered, go through the same process as if you are in a store. Check your "yes" and "no" answers and ask if the pendulum is a good choice for you to work with. If you are buying online, try to purchase from a store with an unequivocal money-back guarantee. In the UK, you have 14 days to return any item bought online for a refund. In the US, it is at the discretion of the online store and not a legal requirement (this is correct at the time of writing, but you should always check the store's return policy before purchasing).

Crystal Colors

Colors are an important part of life. They can affect your mood, lifting you up and calming you down. We choose colors all the time, both consciously and subconsciously. You may, for example, have just grabbed the first item of clothing in your wardrobe one morning, only to find later in the day that it's perfect for an unexpected lunch meeting.

You will notice in the Crystal Finder (see pages 102–39) that several crystals, such as calcite and fluorite, naturally occur in a variety of colors. The colors of a crystal are part of its language and affect its meanings. When you notice a crystal or it jumps out at you, one of the things you will be aware of is its color. For example, all calcites are generally telling you to slow down, relax, and chill out, but they say it in very different ways. Green calcite says, "Don't panic! Stop, breathe, it's not as bad as it seems," whereas orange calcite says, "Don't take it all too seriously and remember to laugh." Both types of calcite are saying the same thing, but they are addressing the issue in very different ways.

WHY DO CRYSTALS CHANGE COLOR?

Some crystals such as amethyst may fade in bright direct sunlight. This is because these crystals have been underground for several hundred million years and they just don't like sunlight. But other crystals can change color as you work with them—the pink color of rose quartz, for example, can fade. Or you may find the colors of certain crystals becoming enhanced or changing. These crystals are shining brighter because they love working with you.

However, just like us, crystals can look faded and dull, losing their shine when they are overworked and underpaid! Sometimes, the color will come back when you cleanse the crystal, but it may be that it needs a rest. In other words, the crystal needs a vacation, just as we do. To do this, simply put the crystal on an amethyst bed or inside an amethyst geode. People often ask me how long they should leave the crystal there. The answer is simple—don't ask me, ask your crystal! After all, sometimes you just need a day by the beach or a weekend city break, but other times a week in the mountains, two weeks in the sun, or a month in the Caribbean is what's required! But you will know the answer just by looking at your crystal every day. One day, you will notice its color has returned and it's bright, sparkly, and ready to go to work again. There are also crystals that change color in different lighting. Usually, these changes are due to pleochroism,

Amethyst bed

CRYSTAL COLORS AND THEIR INFLUENCES

RED
Grounding, awareness, movement, passion, moving forward in life

ORANGE
Energy, creativity, sexuality

YELLOW
Fun, laughter, happiness, intellect, focus of energy

PINK
Connection to people, love, friendship, romance, openness

BLUE
Communication, calmness, stillness

INDIGO
Intuition, awareness, spirit communication, angels

WHITE
Purity, stillness, clarity of thought, cleansing

CLEAR
Healing, intuition, connection, amplification, clarity

BLACK
Grounding, protection, deflecting, promoting change, mystery

BROWN
Earth, friendship, animals

MULTICOLORED
Seeing things from different angles, free thinking, confrontation

GREEN
Calming, success, healing,
emotion, plants, nature

VIOLET
Spirituality, imagination,
connection to spirit

GRAY
Intelligence, sadness, safety

RAINBOW-COLORED
Opportunities, possibilities, fresh
start, potential

which is where crystals change color when viewed from different angles, as is the case with tanzanite and some tourmaline crystals. Rarely, a color change is seen when there is a change in the light source, such as from daylight, incandescent light from lamps with tungsten light bulbs, and candle flames. This phenomemon is a feature of alexandrite, which is a variety of chrysoberyl.

Always take notice when your crystal changes color because of an optical or energetic effect. If you are unsure what the crystal is trying to say to you, ask your crystal pendulum for help (see page 25).

Tanzanite

Tourmaline

exercise: SENSING CRYSTAL COLORS

A fun exercise you can do with a friend is to collect a group of the same variety of crystal that occurs in different colors, such as calcite in its red, orange, gold, green, blue, and pink forms. You will need an identical opaque container for each crystal (an envelope or covered wooden bowl both work well for smaller crystals). So, for this exercise, you will need six containers.

1 Ask your friend to hide one crystal in each container and close or cover these, so you cannot see which is which.
2 Pass your dominant hand over each container and see if you can sense the differences in the energies of the crystals.
3 Once you notice a difference between the containers, try to identify which color is hidden in each one. The darker colors will have the "heavier" energy. Then, swap over and let your friend also try the same exercise.

Note: If you are having difficulty sensing the energy, shake your hands vigorously for a minute or so, then immediately try the exercise again. This movement gets more blood into your hands and helps to make the nerves more sensitive to energy.

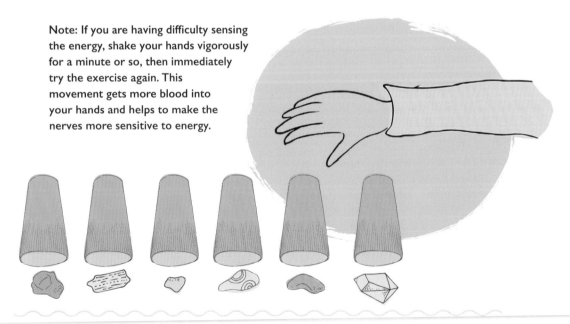

meditation: LISTEN TO YOUR CRYSTALS

Meditation is a core practice of all spiritual traditions around the world. It can help you with almost anything by altering the way your mind sees the world and processes information. For this meditation, you can work with any one of your crystals, but you might find clear quartz is the easiest to work with.

1   Start with the Meditation Preparation that you discovered earlier in the chapter (see page 18).

2   Now, hold your crystal in your left hand and spend a little time just looking at and exploring it. Close your eyes. As you breathe in, imagine you are breathing in the color of the crystal in the form of a bright light. If the crystal is colorless, like clear quartz, then you will see a bright white light emanating from the crystal.

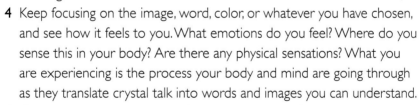

3   Watch the light of the crystal as it comes in through your closed eyes and starts to fill your mind. As it does so, start noticing that the light in your mind contains lots of different things. These might be images, words, colors, ideas, or anything you see there. Focus on the brightest or clearest one.

4   Keep focusing on the image, word, color, or whatever you have chosen, and see how it feels to you. What emotions do you feel? Where do you sense this in your body? Are there any physical sensations? What you are experiencing is the process your body and mind are going through as they translate crystal talk into words and images you can understand.

5   Once you have explored this first image or word, for example, open your awareness again and focus on the next thing you see in your mind. Repeat this process for as long as you like.

6   When you have finished, take a few slow, deep breaths in through your nose and out through your mouth. Open your eyes and slowly bring your focus back into the room. It may take several meditation sessions to see all that the crystal is trying to tell you.

Chapter Two

YOUR CRYSTAL FRIENDS

Have you ever found yourself talking to your crystals? Crazy?
Well, we'll explore this next to open your heart and mind to the view
that crystals are really speaking to you. Do you choose crystals, or do they
choose you? And what makes some crystals special to you rather than
others. Then you will see how to use all your senses to discover the
crystals you really need.

Am I Crazy to Talk to My Crystals?

Not at all! Remember in the first chapter we discovered that many biologists believe crystals are alive (see page 11)? Well, we talk to our pets and some people talk to all manner of animals and plants. So, how is talking to crystals any different? Really, talking to crystals is only a problem if someone doesn't understand that they are, in fact, considered to be living, eating, growing, and reproducing life forms.

Humans tend to reject anything different, and yet humanity is the very force that accepts diversity in all its forms. Rejection of difference creates turmoil and wars, while acceptance creates love and peace. Crystals are part of this worldwide expanse of love and peace. They are friends and allies with a message to help us on our way.

FINDING YOUR SPECIAL CRYSTAL FRIEND

You might be surprised when you find your special crystal friend because it will suddenly, and sometimes unexpectedly, jump out at you. Sometimes, it will literally jump! I've even seen crystals jump off a shelf as a customer has been looking at them.

With some relationships it's love at first sight, while with others you may need to work at your connection together. The same is true for crystals. There is a special one that will always be there for you, but how do you find it?

The first time I went crystal shopping, I was struck by the energy, the magnetic pull of so many crystals in one place. So, how do you go about finding your special crystal? Well, if you listen to your inner pendulum (see page 24), it will guide you. If you think you will need help with this, then it's always a good idea to take your crystal pendulum with you. Open your eyes and your heart and let yourself be drawn to the crystals you need.

Whenever you are uncertain about a crystal, simply hold it in your hand, hold your crystal pendulum over it, and ask your pendulum if this is a good crystal for you to work with. If the crystal is too big to hold, then just touch it and look at it as you ask your question. Crystals can also predict things to come. So, it is also worth asking if you will need this crystal in the future.

Lapis lazuli pendulum

THERE'S A CRYSTAL FRIEND FOR EVERYONE

Let me tell you a story. One day, I remember a large family group coming into my store on a day out and each person chose a crystal except for the father, who was a complete sceptic. However, the family wanted him to have a crystal too, so they asked me to choose one for him. The moment I agreed, a small citrine tumble polished stone shone out from across the store. I retrieved the citrine, gave it to the father, and explained I felt very strongly that this crystal was for his gut, something to do with digestion. He explained that he had never had any problems with his stomach and didn't need it. I suggested that sometimes crystals can be predictive and he could take the citrine as a gift, as long as he promised to let me know what happened with it, and he agreed. The family went off for the rest of their day out. Early the next day, the father phoned me—he was flabbergasted! They had met some friends in town and gone for a meal. Everyone got food poisoning except for him! He is no longer sceptical about crystals. To discover how to hear and connect with your special crystal friends, try the Open Your Heart exercise (see page 46).

Citrine

QUARTZ MASTER CRYSTALS

Quartz is known as the *master healer*. This is because it can channel any type of energy and help all situations and conditions on every level, physical, mental, emotional, and spiritual. Whenever a crystal healer has not got the perfect crystal for a specific disorder, they always fall back on quartz. It may not be the best crystal for a particular issue, but it will always help.

Sooner or later, you will find your quartz master crystal. These crystals might not seem anything special until you find the right one for you. What makes this quartz a master crystal? Well, this is subjective, but a quartz master crystal will fit in your hand and it will be the one you don't want to put down. The one that feels as if it has always been yours. It is the one that chooses you. It's the quartz crystal that makes the hairs on your arms stand on end or sends shivers down your spine. This crystal will become your lifelong friend. Whether for healing yourself or others, for meditation, to provide inspiration, or some or all of these things, this is your master crystal and it will help you with anything you ask for.

When I give crystal healing treatments to clients, there are times when I miss something. I may think I have laid all the crystals on my client that they need, but there can be this nagging feeling at the back of my mind. So, I focus on my quartz master crystal, and he always puts me right. He interprets the words, thoughts, and energies of other crystals that I may otherwise miss. It's like having a translator with me to help me understand the nuances of crystal talk (see page 45).

A Long Time Ago…The Year I Met the Lemurian Quartz Crystals

The Tucson Gem Show, held in Arizona, is a crystal lover's dream. The main show is the Tucson Gem & Mineral Show, which lasts for four days, and there are dozens of shows running for weeks beforehand. It was at one of these shows that I discovered several tables outside in the Tucson winter sunshine covered in the most amazing quartz crystals I had ever seen. They weren't just calling and waving—they were singing and

shouting to me! And they weren't doing this for everyone. Many people were just walking by, as if they hadn't even seen them. As one of the crystals glowed, I picked it up and it shone. Then another and another. I went to pick one up and its bright light faded, as if to say, "No, not me, thanks." So, I left that crystal where it was.

The next thing I realized, these crystals were saying names to me. At first, I thought they were telling me their names, then just random names, until I realized they were my customers' names! Each crystal was telling me who they wanted to work with. Fortunately, I was initiated into the world of Lemurian crystal energy by a shaman who seemed to be hanging around the display tables, and their words became even clearer. There was one crystal that didn't tell me a name, but it did say that it wanted to fly. I was leaving for the UK in a few days, so I thought he wanted to come with me. As I was paying the now rather large bill (!), I put the flying crystal back and left him. I couldn't have told you why either. He was a lovely crystal that had spoken to me. A couple of days later, as I was about to leave for home, I popped by the stand to say farewell and noticed that the flying crystal wasn't there. I asked who had bought him. It was a pilot who was going to keep him in his cabin bag.

Lemurian quartz

So, once I got back to St Albans, in the UK, I decided that as these crystals wanted to be with specific people, I wouldn't put them on display in the store, but keep them upstairs in a storage area instead. All but four of the crystals had told me who they wanted to go to. I called these customers and said there might be a crystal for them. As each customer came in, I invited them to look at the crystals upstairs and left them to choose. None of the crystals was labeled and every one of my customers came back down with the crystal that had spoken their name when I chose them in Tucson. Every now and again, I had a feeling that a new customer was destined for one of the other four crystals and asked if they'd like to see them. They too came down with one of the four crystals and never chose one destined for someone else.

Over the last 20 years, since I discovered Lemurian quartz crystals, I have learned so much from these amazing crystal friends and continue to do so to this today. In fact, each time I teach my "Lemurian Crystal Workshop," it is always a little different, as these crystals show me the next step on my journey.

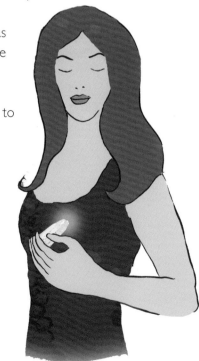

exercise:
CHOOSING YOUR QUARTZ MASTER CRYSTAL

Your quartz master crystal is one of the most important crystals you will have, so be patient and take your time selecting it. The selection process below can be very exciting as you are feeling the crystal's energy. Remember to breathe and take your time—this should not be rushed..

1 Find a place, such as a crystal store, with a selection of quartz crystals. Which quartz crystal are you drawn to? It might be the brightest, shiniest, biggest, smallest, smartest, or oddest, but it will always be the one that stands out for you. It is the one doing the crystal equivalent of jumping up and down, shouting "Me! Me! Me!!" and waving at you!

2 Pick this crystal up and hold it for a moment. If it feels as if it is losing its connection, or the brightness is fading or the sparkle lessening, put it back and start again. There is nothing wrong, but the crystal just thought you were someone else. It happens.

3 Assuming you still have the crystal, hold it in your dominant hand with the termination pointing to the open palm of your other hand. Slowly move the crystal in clockwise circles. You will feel a "pull." Some people describe this as heat or coolness, pressure, or a tingling sensation on the skin, a little like pins and needles. If you experience any of these or something similar, then this is the crystal for you.

4 Depending on where you have found this crystal, you may want to cleanse it.

Cleansing Crystals

Cleansing is the process of spiritual or energetic cleaning. Although this can include washing a crystal, the intention is to remove unhelpful or unwanted energies. Some people like to call these negative energies, but I prefer to avoid this term as it has many connotations that may or may not be valid at those times you would like to cleanse your crystal. However, a good example of a situation in which you may want to cleanse a crystal is when you've been introducing friends to the idea of crystals and healing. Perhaps you have passed the crystal around for everyone to feel its energy, but you then want to work with the crystal yourself and don't want others' influence. Your friends' energy is not negative or bad; it is just not yours. Cleansing your crystal using one of the methods on pages 40–42 will help refresh and restore it.

WHY DO CRYSTALS NEED CLEANSING?

Whenever you work with crystals or just hold them, play, or meditate with them, or carry them in your pocket, for example, there is an exchange of energy. The crystal gives you some power and you give the crystal power in return, often releasing energy you no longer need. This may be related to a physical injury or disease or a past trauma that has affected you in an emotional, mental, or spiritual way.

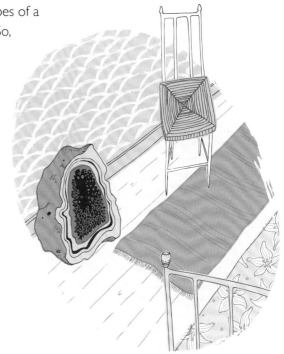

Crystals will also sometimes pick up the vibes of a disagreement that has taken place in a room. So, even if you're just having a bad day, hold your crystal and you will feel better. The crystal will draw out the energy that is upsetting your balance, replacing it with a fresh vibrant crystalline power within you.

You can see and feel when crystals need cleansing because they will appear dull, as if they've lost some of their sparkle or shine. When you hold them, they can feel a little tacky or gunky, as if they need a wash.

CRYSTAL CLEANSING METHODS

It is important to clearly focus your mind and intent for all spiritual cleansing techniques. This is because your intent is amplified and focused with all these practices. You can cleanse your crystals using the following methods:

Sound

This is my go-to method of cleansing. As you can probably imagine, I have a lot of crystals, so if I cleansed them with running water from a mountain stream, I would spend all my time running up and down mountains! My preferred instrument for sound cleansing is the tingsha. These are made from two small cymbals that are tied together, usually with a strip of leather. They are traditionally made of seven different metals (sometimes five) and when struck together the sound waves bounce back and forth through the different metals. They can ring for ages.

All matter vibrates. You do, the chair you are sitting on does, as does the air you breathe and your crystals. It is this sound vibration that literally shakes the unwanted energy from the crystals and cleanses them. You can also use tingsha to cleanse your aura, your personal sacred space, your home, car, office, or anywhere you wish. Chanting and drumming can also produce cleansing sound vibrations.

Running Water

To cleanse a crystal, simply hold it under running water. If you live at the top of a mountain, then there's nothing fresher than stream water, but it is best to avoid water lower down, as it may have been polluted by animals. Fortunately, you can just use water from your tap! If you want to clean lots of crystals at the same time, pop them in a colander or sieve and cleanse them together under the tap.

Some crystals are not suitable for this method as they are either water soluble so will dissolve. Also be careful with crystals like celestite that have a sandy matrix, as they may fall apart. Also avoid the vortex healing crystal, copper, malachite, selenite, and celestite.

Smudging

The smoke from sage and a few other natural sources, such as sandalwood, frankincense, and Palo Santo, can be used to cleanse crystals, as well as your aura and home. Sage is often used by North America's First Nation peoples, sandalwood is common in Eastern traditions and frankincense in the West, and Palo Santo is the traditional choice in some areas of South America. They all have the same cleansing effects, with the choice of what to use no doubt dictated by local availability in different regions.

The First Nations' smudging ceremony varies from one Nation to another, but essentially involves a smudge stick (which is a sage bundle), a large seashell dish (usually an abalone shell), and a feather to direct the smoke and carry your prayers to spirit. To conduct a ceremony, light the sage bundle and immediately blow it out, leaving it to smoke. Hold the sage bundle over the shell dish to catch the embers and then direct the smoke over the crystal, or whatever you are cleansing, with the feather. The ceremony combines the power of the four elements to add strength to the intention, with the sage representing Earth; the feather, Air; the smoke, Fire; and the shell, Water. This creates a very powerful cleansing energy that is full of intent.

Moonlight

Many people like to experience the ritual of cleansing crystals under a full moon. To do this, take the crystals outside, arrange them in your backyard, and sit with them for a while, meditating as you bathe with them in the silvery moonlight. If you don't have a backyard, use a windowsill or a suitable outdoor place. Maybe you can meet up with a few friends for a crystal cleansing party.

The Moon's energy affects us all and our crystals anyway, but adding your intent makes the whole cleansing process so much more powerful. Why not make it a regular ritual each month?

Rebirth

This is a ritual of burying your crystal in the ground and digging it up later when it will be born afresh. A good time to bury crystals is during a full moon and they should be dug up again at the following new moon, which is the time of new beginnings. Again, if you don't have a backyard, you can use a windowbox or plant pot.

Selenite

Working With Other Crystals

You can also work with other crystals, such as selenite, amethyst, carnelian, and quartz, to cleanse crystals. Place the crystal on a flat piece of selenite, either on a plate or in a bowl, and leave overnight. You can also pop a carnelian in your pocket, bra, or a pouch, or wherever you keep your crystals on you. Alternatively, place the crystals on a large amethyst bed or inside a geode to give them a vacation (see page 27). Or put them on a quartz crystal bed overnight to re-energize them for the morning.

Amethyst

Please note that all crystals need cleansing (regardless of their own cleansing powers)—even those employed to cleanse other crystals. To do this, simply use one of the other crystal cleansing methods.

Breath

The breath can also be used to cleanse crystals. Hold the crystal that needs cleansing and still your mind. Focus on the crystal and letting go of anything that is unhelpful for you and the crystal. Take a deep breath right down into your stomach and keep inhaling to fill your lungs. Pause for a moment, focus on the crystal, then exhale across it, blowing any unwanted energy away.

Carnelian

DON'T USE SALT TO CLEANSE CRYSTALS

Articles on the internet and some books by "experts" suggest you can cleanse crystals with salt, but here are three reasons why you should avoid this:

- **Salt is a crystal (halite)** When you put a crystal in salt, you are rubbing two crystals together: your crystal and halite. As you do this, the softer crystal will be damaged. Most of the time this will be the halite. However, crystals such as celestite and selenite will become scratched and dull and lose their sparkle. Additionally, crystals like vortex healing crystal and chalcopyrite have a surface color due to oxidation that might be lost in this process.
- **Salt water drains energy** If you give salt water an electrical charge, you set up a battery because the positive sodium and negative chlorine ions in the salt move to their opposite poles. As we will see in Chapter 3, crystals have an electrical charge, so if you put a crystal in salt water, you create a battery in the same way. Leave the crystal there and it will run flat. This is the only way I have ever found to take all the life from a quartz crystal.
- **Salt is unpleasant** Finally, if you asked a friend to help you fix your car and they got a bit mucky under the hood, would you say, "Thank you, would you like a bath of cold salt water?" I think not. You are more likely to offer your friend a warm shower or a bubble bath. Crystals love bubble baths too! If you treat your crystals as friends, you won't go far wrong.

Do You Choose Crystals— or Do They Choose You?

I have already touched on the idea that crystals may choose us, rather than the other way round, but let's look at this in more detail and examine what is happening when you "select" a crystal. Firstly, we should consider how crystals exist and recognize that they are living according to a different time scale to us (see page 11). Most crystals are millions, hundreds of millions, or even billions of years old. For example, the popular quartz and amethyst crystals from Brazil were all well formed by the time the Jurassic dinosaurs walked the Earth. We often think of dinosaur fossils (organic matter turned to stone) as "old" and yet they are perhaps some of the children of the mineral world, with their great-great-great-grandparents being the amethyst and quartz crystals growing beneath their feet. And their ancestors are billions of years old. The human mind cannot begin to comprehend such vast time scales. Their amazing wealth of millions of years of experience tells them when to turn on their crystal charms, such as just catching the light and sparkling or brightening their colour, at the very moment you walk past them.

Another question: are we governed by fate, or do we have free will? What does that have to do with crystals, I hear you ask? Well, if everything is predetermined, then you were always going to find that crystal, your paths inexplicably intertwined through billions of years. Or, if you have free will, then, of course, you can choose whichever crystal you find draws you or is attractive to you. Although I don't know the definitive answer to this age-old question, I do believe we have choice. Except, then we must ask why we find a particular crystal attractive? Is it the brightest color or the perfect shade for you, or perhaps the sparkliest, largest, or most delicate?

 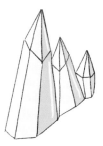   

CRYSTAL COMMUNICATION

Earlier in this chapter, I related the story of how I was introduced to Lemurian quartz crystals (see pages 36–37). If you remember, some of them drew me in different ways. Occasionally, one shone brightly and I found it very attractive, but then it would suddenly go dull, as if it was hiding and didn't want to come with me.

In the same way, I've seen groups of people look at a shelf of similar crystals and each person only sees one or two crystals. And these are always different to the ones noticed by their friends. The light has not changed, the crystals haven't moved, and people are standing in the same area, and yet different crystals are looking bright and calling out to different people. I have even seen crystals wink and sparkle, heard them call out, felt their need to be with me or for me to carry them to who they want to be with. So, perhaps it is the crystals choosing us after all.

CRYSTAL SPEAK

Understanding what our crystals are trying to tell us can be baffling. It's just like learning a foreign language: you study hard and learn all the words, but you might not pronounce them properly and will miss colloquialisms in everyday conversations. On the other hand, if you read the books and then go and live in that country, you quickly learn to speak like a native, picking up the local dialect and accent too. The same is true with crystals. You can read all the crystal books you like, and many contain very helpful information, but you need to work on yourself and others with crystals.

You need crystals around you all the time, so you can interact with them when you're feeling happy and when you're feeling low. There will be times when you need a little help from your crystal friends to get through the day or a sparkle of inspiration for your latest idea or project. When you need to take the edge off your pain or calm you to sleep if your mind won't rest. If you think this sounds like a chemical-induced utopia, it can be. It is about "being" and experiencing every day and asking your crystal friends for a little help when you need it. You may have big flashes of "wowness" with your crystals—and these are amazing—but it is the mundane things that will show what your crystals are telling you every day.

exercise: OPEN YOUR HEART

Opening your heart and mind to the possibility that crystals are trying to communicate with us can be one of the most difficult aspects of working with crystals for some people. Even those trained to look at life with an open mind sometimes find it difficult. This is a simple experiment you can do at home with whatever crystals you have to help you open your heart to the crystals that are trying to communicate with you.

1 Place all your crystals (or just some of them if you have a lot) around you. You can do this while sitting on the floor or in a chair. First, do your Meditation Preparation (see page 18).

2 In your mind, imagine there is a pink loving energy in your heart. As you continue to breathe, breathe in a green energy. Watch the green and pink energies mix like interweaving ribbons on a maypole. When you feel ready, imagine these ribbons coming out of your heart and touching one of the crystals around you. Which crystal has it connected with? How does this connection feel? Did anything surprise you?

3 Repeat this process as many times as you like and notice the crystals you connect with and how each one makes you feel.

4 When you open your heart and make connections, whether with crystals or people, beautiful things can happen. We all hear, we all interact with natural energies, but sometimes we just don't listen.

What Makes Some Crystals Special to Me?

It is often not just one variety of crystal that draws you, but a specific crystal which calls to you above all the others. But what makes this crystal so special? Here are some things to look out for:

- Brightness in or around the crystal
- Sparkles in or on the crystal
- Vivid colors in the crystal or your mind
- Gentle, soothing hues in the crystal or your mind
- Rainbows in the crystal
- Faces, spirits, or animals appearing in the inclusions or faults in a crystal
- A feeling of not being alone, as if someone is there with you
- Heat, coolness, or tingly feelings in your hands when you hold the crystal
- Heat, coolness, or tingly feelings anywhere in your body when you hold or look at the crystal
- The crystal feeling unusually heavy or light in your hand
- An overwhelming feeling of love or peace
- The hairs standing up on your arms or the back of your neck
- A shiver running up or down your spine
- A spark of electricity from the crystal when you touch it, which feels like a small electric shock
- A word or words that pop into your head

exercise:
USING YOUR SENSES TO CHOOSE CRYSTALS

We looked at using all the five senses to explore a crystal in Chapter 1 (see Sensing Crystal Energy, pages 16–17). Now, let's use our senses again in this fun and informative exercise, which is lovely to do with a friend. Practice the exercise at home and then try it out in your local crystal store.

To prepare, choose some crystals. If you are going to explore your sense of taste (step 5), then ensure the crystals are safe and washed clean. Avoid this step for any crystal that has a "No Elixir" warning (see pages 102–39).

1 **Sight** Close your eyes or wear a blindfold, so you can't peek, and ask your friend to arrange the crystals in front of you. Open your eyes and choose the first one you see. Check its message in the Crystal Finder chapter. Then swap over and let your friend have a go.

2 **Smell** Again, with eyes closed or blindfolded, ask your friend to hand you crystals one at a time in a random order. Smell each one. Take your time if you need to. What do you smell with each one? Crystals do have different fragrances. Don't worry if you cannot identify the specific aromas, as long as you are recognizing that they are there and are different for each variety of crystal. Swap over, so your friend can try this too.

3 **Hearing** Wearing a blindfold or with your eyes closed, ask your friend to hold each crystal near to your ear, 1–2cm (½–1 in.) away. Listen for the vibrations of the crystal. We hear this as sound. Listen carefully and you will notice that different types of crystal sound different. Again, swap over, so your friend can try this as well.

4 **Touch** Sit comfortably with your arms out in front of you and palms raised. Restrict your sight by closing your eyes or wearing a blindfold. Have your friend place different

crystals in your hands, one at a time, so you can explore them with your fingers. I'm always surprised at how this feels so different to touching crystals when you can see them. When you have finished, change places with your friend, so they can also experience this.

5 **Taste** Make sure the crystals are safe and clean. For this reason, it is best to place them on the tip of your tongue yourself. As before, restrict your sight and ask your friend to pass you the crystals one at a time. Hold each crystal to the tip of your tongue until you are aware of a taste. Don't be concerned if you can't describe the taste or if the crystal tastes like something very ordinary. Accept whatever you experience. Swap places with your friend, so they can have a go.

Note: If you don't have a friend with you for this exercise, put tumble polished crystals in a pouch that is large enough for you to get your hand in. Pull each crystal randomly from the pouch with your eyes closed. Cut and polished or rough natural stones may be damaged if shaken in the pouch.

field-of-crystals meditation:
FINDING THE CRYSTALS YOU NEED IN YOUR LIFE

Another way of discovering helpful crystals is through meditation. Here is a guided visualization to help you meet some new crystal friends.

1 Start with the Meditation Preparation that you learned at the start of the book (see page 18). Now continue to breathe comfortably.

2 In your mind, imagine a massive field of crystals. They are like a crop growing in the field, except most of them are different from one another. You have a crystal harvesting bag. Allow yourself to feel from your heart and walk through this field of crystals, going whichever way your heart directs you.

3 Whenever you want to pause in your walk, look at the crystal you stopped by. Which one is it? It doesn't matter if you cannot identify the crystal right now; just pick it up and see if it looks or feels attractive in your hand. In your mind, use all your senses. Be aware of what the crystal looks and feels like, as well as how it smells, sounds, and tastes.

4 Is the crystal you chose speaking to you? How do you feel holding this crystal? Do you want to keep this crystal with you or let it go? If you feel you want to take the crystal with you, it is something you need right now. But if you are uncertain, then take it anyway, as it will be needed in the future.

5 Sometimes you may completely dislike the crystal. This is because crystals can make us feel uncomfortable, as they focus on something we have suppressed and do not want to look at. You should definitely take this crystal with you! These are the life-changing crystals that will help you shed the issues holding you back.

6 To finish, thank your field of crystals and remember that it is always there for you when you need some crystal guidance. The more you practice this field-of-crystals meditation, the easier it will be for you to step in and out of the field as you need to.

Chapter Three
WORKING WITH CRYSTALS

Working with crystals can help you with just about anything you are doing or wish to do. If you treat your crystals as friends and honor the sacredness of Mother Earth, they will help you in more ways than you can imagine. Whether you need help with a physical injury or disease, your mental clarity or health, are experiencing relationship, emotional, or financial upsets and trauma, or seeking spiritual connection and understanding, there are crystals out there for you.

Where Are Crystals Found?

Crystals are found in and on the ground and in the technology all around us. Much of our 21st-century lifestyle is based on crystal technology, and humans have, in fact, been using crystals as tools from the very earliest times (see page 15). Even your body contains an amazing number of crystals, such as calcium crystals to make your teeth and bones strong.

CRYSTALS IN OUR MODERN WORLD

Quartz and tourmaline are the only two materials we know of in the universe that have a solid state electric field. This field stops your computer blowing up when there's a power surge. In fact, it prevents everything with a sensitive electrical circuit that is plugged into mains electricty from blowing up or crashing down around you.

Quartz

Quartz crystals also keep perfect time and are found in watches and clocks, with billions of people relying on their quartz crystal watch every day. There are crystals in your cell phone, TV, electric oven and hob, microwave, dishwasher, washing machine, and tumble dryer. Whether you listen to the radio on a crystal wireless set or digital radio, there's a crystal in there as well! Medical technology is full of crystals too—rubies, for example, are used in X-ray machines. Lasers also rely on crystal technology, with rubies being used for lasers emitting a red laser light (sapphires are used for blue lasers and alexandrite for green). So, if someone says disparagingly that crystals are not exactly rocket science, you can happily correct them, because without crystal technology we would never have reached the Moon or deep space, or even emerged from caves in the first place.

Tourmaline

Today, most people can easily access crystals in crystal stores and gift stores, and through the internet. I always recommend buying from a store in person, but if that is not possible, then buy online from a trusted source.

Ruby

CRYSTALS IN NATURE

You can also find crystals and rocks all around you outdoors. Different areas in different countries naturally have an abundant supply of something geologically wonderful. Check out what occurs naturally in your local area and see if there's a local mine or quarry where you could collect some crystals yourself. You can also find crystals on stony beaches, mountains, and rocky outcrops, and in places where they are building new roads or repairing old ones. If necessary, ask the landowners' consent first when you go hunting for crystals.

CRYSTAL-HUNTING TIPS

If you are going on a crystal-hunting expedition, tell someone where you are going and take the following items with you:

- Sturdy backpack made of tear-resistant material—you're going to be carrying rocks back! Ensure it has large pockets and adjustable straps
- Geological hammer or rock pick (or a hammer and chisel or a hammer with a pointed tip in the head)
- Brushes to remove grime from your crystal finds
- Soft pouch bag, snap-and-seal bags, or plastic containers with lids for collecting your finds
- Protective gloves and safety glasses
- Hardwearing boots and an outer layer of waterproof clothing such as trousers and a jacket
- Headlamp—this is easier than holding a torch—as lots of crystals grow in nooks and cavities
- Water and food, as you will likely be searching in a remote area
- First-aid kit and a fully charged cell phone—just in case

Which Crystals Should I Take Home?

The first thing I do when I find crystals is to ask them if they would like to come with me or stay where they are. And this applies to every situation, whether the crystal is in a store or on a mountain, at a rock show, or in a mine. The crystals you find might be amazing, sparkly, shiny, and stunningly energetic, but sometimes they need to be with someone else. Other times, the crystals want to come with me to reach whoever they need to be with. Occasionally, they are for me.

Connecting with the Crystals You Find

Whenever I come across a crystal or rock that talks to me when I'm out and about, I like to spend a little time with it. You see, once you start listening to crystals, you quickly realize that they're a chatty lot. Not every crystal that says "Hi" wants to come with you, though; sometimes they're just being welcoming to a stranger. I'll pick the crystal up and hold it or maybe pop it in my pocket for a while—don't do this in a store; just keep it in your hand instead. I'll quickly get a sense of whether the stone wants to do something or stay where it is. The crystal is either left in the same place or, if I feel this is needed, moved a short distance from where it was found. Now and then, my new rock friend will want a chat, imparting a morsel of knowledge or wisdom about a situation, and, very occasionally, will want to come with me on my journey.

I believe we find crystals either when we need them for ourselves, or they may be for a customer, colleague, friend, or relative. It is not uncommon for each of us to become a facilitator in this way, helping others on their path through life.

Should I Cleanse My New Crystals?

Some people say you should always cleanse new crystals, but I don't agree. I'm sure crystals should sometimes be cleansed as soon as you get home, but at other times, this really isn't necessary and possibly even ill-advised. Here are some scenarios to get you thinking:

- You are in a store you do not frequent regularly. You feel uneasy about something, but you are not sure what. You are drawn to a crystal. It looks amazing, and it's waving and jumping up and down, saying: "Take me home!" You buy the crystal and once out of the store, you feel relieved. Cleanse this crystal as soon as you get home. There is something about the store or someone in the store that is not good for you, but you have found a lovely new crystal.

- You buy a selection of crystals from a happy store. Everything feels great, but when you get home, you notice that one crystal looks dull compared to how bright it was in the store. This crystal has probably picked up some unhelpful energy from another customer. This happens all the time. It is not necessarily bad or negative energy, but it is energy you do not need. Remember that every time anyone interacts with a crystal, whether consciously or not, there is an exchange of energy. So, cleanse this crystal. Of course, you can cleanse all the crystals you buy if you wish.
- You are out and about hunting for rocks and find some very interesting crystals. These have come from the Earth and probably won't need cleansing immediately. However, you will probably want to wash them before taking them home.

Salt crystal from the Dead Sea, Israel

- You are walking in the countryside or on a beach, and you find a sparkly stone that's talking to you. Again, you probably do not need to cleanse this.

- You have bought some crystals online from someone you don't know. In this instance, you should always cleanse them on receipt. If you're buying from a trusted source, see how they feel to you and cleanse any or all of them if you wish.

- You have bought a crystal for someone else. Here, I always advise not to cleanse the crystal. If you have gone to a store specifically with your friend in mind, then the crystals will respond to your intention. Many times, I have seen a customer come into the store looking for a gift and say something like: "I really like that crystal, but I'm not sure my friend will." My advice is always the same. Take yourself out of the scenario and think about who the crystal is for. Focus on them, hold a picture of them in your mind (or look at a photo on your cell phone), and tune in to their energy. Then start looking again. Your friend will always choose something different. This crystal is not for you, but as you've tuned in to the energy of the person it is for, it is up to them to cleanse the crystal. You may feel the crystal needs cleansing because it has an energy that is not yours—you were obviously focusing on the final receiver's energy and not your own. If, when you get home, the crystal feels uncomfortable for you, pop it in a sealed plastic bag until you can pass it on. Plastic significantly reduces the transfer of many subtle energies.

Any time you are unsure what to do, you can always ask your crystal pendulum. As I've already mentioned, the more you check with your pendulum, the more you will learn to trust your intuition and inner pendulum (see Connecting with Crystal Friends Using a Pendulum, page 23).

Welcoming New Crystals into Your Home

Whether you have bought your crystals in a store, purchased them online, or found them in nature, you need to welcome them into your home. Take a quiet moment to unpack them. Ask them if they're happy and let them breathe. Don't worry if you have a little difficulty feeling or hearing these crystals: the more you keep an open mind with crystals around you, the more you will understand what they are telling you. Always be aware of all your senses— hearing, sight, smell, taste, and touch. All of us sense differently, and express our experiences in our own unique way, none of which are wrong. Take your time and explore each of your new crystals with all your senses, if it is safe to do so (see Using Your Senses to Choose Crystals, page 48). You might want to cleanse the crystals too, if you feel they need it (see Cleansing Crystals, page 39).

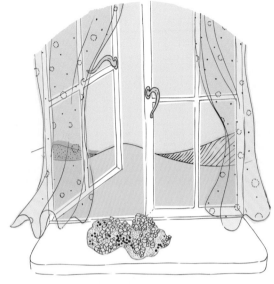

When you are ready, let the crystals get to know their new home and the other crystals you already have around. You might feel they want to be together or separate, near other crystals or not. Trust your feelings and, if you are uncertain, remember you can always ask your pendulum to help. You might notice the crystals become brighter or their color more pronounced. When your crystals are happy, they will be more ready to help you.

NEW CRYSTALS: PRACTICES TO AVOID

There are a few common practices that are far from essential, namely charging, dedicating, and programming new crystals. Although it is fine to try these, I would like you to consider why you are doing them and what happens when you do. Let's look at each practice in turn:

Charging

I've heard and read many times that you should charge crystals when you first get them. When asked why this needs to be done, the answer is usually that the crystals are depleted. However, the crystals had enough energy to attract you and talk to you in the first place. They do not deplete their energy. A basic fact of the Universe is that energy cannot be created or destroyed. It can only be converted from one type to another. People also sometimes say: "Oh, but the crystals might have collected a lot of negative energy." Well, if that was the case, then why were you drawn to that crystal—surely you would have left it well alone?

Let your crystal get to know its friends

Dedicating

Also known as consecrating, dedicating a crystal is a way of saying that it is special and will only work for you. However, I believe all crystals are special, not just the ones that choose to work with me. Dedicating a crystal is, for me, an orthodox approach and a way of limiting the potential of a crystal. When you avoid the error of confining the crystal to your own desires, you can be a heretic and allow yourself and the crystal to be free. You will then find it has so much more potential to help you in ways you couldn't even imagine. I don't want you to be confused by my choice of words. "Orthodox" here means narrow-minded and "heretic" free-thinking. I like crystals to be free, so they can fully and positively express their potential.

Programming

Crystals can be programmed in two ways, one of which is planned and one accidental. When you deliberately program a crystal, you are making it better at a specific thing you want it to do. There are many ways of doing this, but it usually involves concentrating on the crystal in some way, such as during meditation, or consciously focusing and asking or telling the crystal what you want from it. Although this approach will work and make the crystal better at the specific thing you are asking for, it will also reduce its potential to do anything else.

On the other hand, when you simply work with a crystal and do the same thing repeatedly, both the crystal and you will get better at working as a team. It is the same for many of the things we do. For example, anyone can learn to play a musical instrument, but it takes repetition and practice to become proficient. So, if you want to work with a quartz crystal as a master healer crystal (see page 36), for example, then you need to practice healing with it. Both of you will improve each time you see another client or do a treatment on a friend or relative. The crystal will get to know how you heal, how you work, and will support that, and it will also guide you along your path.

You will find yourself trying things you didn't know that you knew—your clients will get better and better treatments and you will not limit your crystal to just being a master healer crystal either. It will be only too pleased to work with you in any way it can, doing anything you ask because it always wants to do amazing things to help you and not just what you have told it to. This also applies to the age of crystals, which I explain on page 11, their time scale, and their deep and ancient wisdom. Treat them as friends and they will support you in more ways than you can ever dream of.

Although it is not wrong to program a crystal, I believe it is an over-simplified way of looking at crystal work and how you can apply the various methods of working with crystals positively, to reach both your crystals' and your own fullest potential.

How to Work with Crystals

There are many ways of working with crystals. I will highlight some of them here, but please don't feel limited to these. Try lots of different methods and find those that work best for you.

CARRY CRYSTALS WITH YOU

This may seem obvious, but it is amazing how many people don't carry crystals with them every day. There are two simple rules to bear in mind here regarding crystals and their energetic interactions:

- **Crystals are always working** If there are crystals near you, they will influence you in a positive way—usually at about 1m (3ft) away if they are new to you. The more you work with the same crystals, and the more you are around them, the larger the area they can affect.

- **Crystals work better with human or animal touch** There are many theories as to why physical contact with crystals is so important. Most of these are too complex for the purposes of the book, but they include pyroelectric and piezoelectric effects, Heisenberg's uncertainty principle and/or the related observer effect, intelligent learning, energy, vibrations, the placebo effect, and more. I have my own personal theory regarding the touch effect, which relates to light and dark matter (see the Dark Matter and Dark Energy box, overleaf). Irrespective of how this is happening, there is a multitude of observed evidence that cannot be ignored.

In short, crystals work better when they have contact with your body or aura. So, if you wear a crystal pendant round your neck, earrings in your ears, or bracelets on your wrists, they will work better than if they are just sitting on a table. If you carry them in your pocket, bra, or in a neck pouch, they will work just as well as in jewelry. If you hold a crystal or balance it on a chakra on your body, or anywhere else, again it will work better.

DARK MATTER AND ENERGY

Dark matter makes up the vast majority of matter in the universe. It is the missing spark that allows gravity to work and hence holds the universe together. You can think of it poetically as the thing that stops you floating off into space and suffocating in the vacuum the moment you are born.

Richard Feynman famously said, "If you think you understand quantum mechanics, you don't understand quantum mechanics." And this is similarly true of dark matter, which may well make quantum mechanics work. As it is made of "dark" and not light (like the world we can see), we can't see it, or sense it, or identify it directly. "Dark" is not a comment on darkness, evil, or negativity in any way; it's just that we cannot see it.

But it affects everything we do. In fact, it may make up 60–95 percent of the universe (along with dark energy). However, it may surprise you to know that many spiritual traditions have always known what it is, and call it by many names such as chi, prana, universal life force, the Tao, the Field, even the Force if you like…It is likely the stuff your soul or spirit is made of, which lives on after your physical body ceases to function.

A large part of you and me and our Stone People friends could be made of dark matter. And this changes everything about the way we respond to them, how they heal us, and how they can communicate with us. Maybe, as you become more aware of the extremities of your senses, you start to become aware of the dark matter in your universe.

WHICH CRYSTALS SHOULD I WORK WITH?

The crystal you need can change many times during the day. This is because as one crystal starts to provide healing, the situation can shift and you may need another to support or replace the first. All crystal healing is a little like peeling an onion: peel off one layer and there is another one underneath. It is a continuous process. You may find that you need the same crystal or group of crystals for a few days or weeks before things start to change. But you will know when they have because the crystals you choose will naturally change. And then… there is another layer…and another…and another layer of your healing onion.

   Start each day by picking one or a few of the crystals you are drawn to and keep them with you throughout the day. Don't worry about why or what these crystals mean. I like to check this at the end of the day if I'm not sure, so the information does not influence the day's events and I can compare my choice of crystals to what actually happened to me.

KEEP CRYSTALS AROUND YOU

Wherever I am, I like to keep a handy selection of crystals nearby. I never know when I'll be drawn to something that will inspire or heal me, or just make me laugh. My crystals always have an answer, even if I'm not certain what the question is. Think about where you spend your time, perhaps in your favorite armchair or at one end of the sofa, at the kitchen table or maybe in bed. It might be your office or another workplace or perhaps your car or truck. It could be an art or music studio, your treatment room, or your meditation or yoga space. When you are relaxing in a bathtub filled with scented bubbles, add your favorite rose quartz crystals to create a topical bathing elixir (see page 20). In other words, you can have crystals anywhere!

exercise: PLACE CRYSTALS ON THE BODY

All crystals are healing, and you can place them anywhere on the body that needs healing. For this method of working with crystals, we usually also focus on the chakras and aura—you can learn about this in the next chapter (see pages 77–83)—but first I want to introduce you to the idea of letting the crystals tell you where to place them. Try this intuitive crystal healing on yourself first. Once you start to feel confident with the process, you can see how it works with other people.

On Yourself

1 Think about healing yourself and choose one crystal that you are drawn to. If you are unsure what you are sensing, then ask your crystal pendulum to help (see page 23). Do your Meditation Preparation (see page 18) before starting.

2 Then hold the crystal and allow your mind to focus on your body. Where is your focus drawn to? Once you recognize an area, place the crystal on or next to this location.

3 Close your eyes again and relax. You can stay like this for as long as you like, but I suggest trying for 5–10 minutes to begin with. Be aware of what you are feeling, not just in that area but also anywhere else in or around your body.

4 You can repeat this with as many crystals as you like, but starting with just one is a good idea, so you can easily focus on what is happening. After a few tries, you can add one or two more crystals and see what happens. Follow the same procedure.

On a Friend

1 When you feel confident, you can start to work on other people. Try sitting with a friend and seeing if you can sense which crystals they need and where to place them.

2 Sit quietly and ask your quartz master crystal to help you intuitively identify your friend's crystal needs. You might be surprised what you start to feel and how quickly this crystal speaks to you—your quartz master crystal can be your translator of crystal speak. If you have any doubts, you can always check any feelings that come up with your pendulum.

3 There are two simple ways to work out where the crystals need to go on your friend. Firstly, you can look at the chakra system and select a crystal for each of the chakras (see pages 77–83). In this scenario, the placement is predetermined, and you will have at least seven crystals, one for each chakra. You can use more crystals if you feel they are needed. Alternatively, you can dowse your friend's body with your pendulum, imagining there is a grid or transparent graph paper above it, with vertical parallel lines running up the body and horizontal lines running across. Hold one of the crystals you have chosen in your nondominant hand and focus on where this crystal should be placed. Move your pendulum up over the midline of their body and stop when you see your positive "yes" movement. Then repeat the process along the corresponding horizontal line.

4 During this process, it is important that you work with a crystal pendulum, holding the crystal you have selected and keeping your quartz master crystal nearby. These crystals will be interacting.

WORK WITH CRYSTALS IN ART

Crystals are sometimes called nature's art and it is easy to see why, because they are beautiful natural creations. You can also add crystals to your own art projects. Whether in the form of small crystals, tumble polished stones, gemstones, or crystal dust, you can build them into creations, stick them on, or sew them in. Maybe you are making a statement piece for a special occasion or want to add some pyrite dust to bring a sparkle to your painting. Crystals can inspire and bring life to a project.

WORK WITH ELIXIRS

Elixir means "miracle substance." By placing a crystal in water and leaving it for a period you can create a miraculous healing liquid. Some elixirs should be drunk, such as those made from amber, which is effective for relieving constipation. Others such as rose quartz make ideal topical elixirs for external use, this one improving your complexion.

Amber

An elixir is a miracle substance

Always be careful here, as some crystals such as selenite can be damaged by water or break down or release toxic elements, as is the case with malachite. The crystals in the Crystal Finder (see pages 102–39) that carry the "No Elixir" warning should be excluded from any water or tasting exercise.

Rose quartz

When you create an elixir by putting a crystal in water, you set up an energy pattern in the water that is unique to the variety of crystal. Amethyst creates amethyst elixir, quartz creates quartz elixir, and so on, and they are all physically different. There is a Japanese theory known as Hado which suggests that beauty creates beauty. As the late Dr Masaru Emoto said: "Hado creates words. Words are the vibrations of nature. Therefore, beautiful words create beautiful nature. Ugly words create ugly nature." Dr Emoto pioneered this field scientifically, showing clearly and photographically that water holds the essence, the feeling of whatever is applied to it—not just through words like love and hate, but also because of any object, such as different crystals, placed in or near the water.

To make an elixir, choose your crystal, then cleanse and wash it (see page 39). Pop the cleansed crystal in a glass or pitcher (jug) of water, then cover and leave in the fridge overnight. If you do not like fridge-cold water, then leave the elixir on the countertop overnight and make sure it is well covered. You can drink the newly made elixir throughout the following day. Then take the same crystal, cleanse and wash it as before, and it will be ready to go in some fresh water the next evening.

Few people realize that crystals can talk to your insides when their energy is consumed in an elixir. We are made up of around 60 percent water, so by regularly drinking an elixir, you will slowly align your body to the specific crystal's energy. This can have a profound effect on your health and happiness.

meditation:
CONNECT WITH YOUR CRYSTAL'S SPIRIT

Meditation is an ancient spiritual practice which has been adapted exceptionally well to help you deal with modern-day stresses. It is also one of the easiest ways to start connecting with crystals. Employ an aqua aura crystal for this meditation. This is a beautiful crystal that combines the energies of quartz crystal with pure gold. Aqua aura has many attributes, one of which is that it can help you connect with spirit and might be the easiest crystal to start with for this exercise.

Aqua aura

As with many of the meditations in this book, once you have practiced and feel more confident, you can enjoy this meditation with lots of different crystals until you have tried it with all the crystals in your collection.

1   Prepare yourself by doing your Meditation Preparation (see page 18).
2   Open your eyes and pick up your aqua aura crystal. See its blueness and take a few breaths, each time breathing this blueness right down into your stomach, completely filling your being with blue aqua aura energy.
3   Now close your eyes and imagine you are slowly shrinking—you are getting smaller, much, much, much smaller until there is a tiny you, looking up at this great big blue aqua aura crystal.
4   You notice a doorway at the bottom of the crystal and make your way over to it. Entering the crystal, you find yourself in a translucent blue world where, despite the luminousness, everything seems oddly very real and solid.
5   Take a few deep breaths, allowing yourself to inhale some of this inner blue luminescence all the way down into your stomach. As you do, you are physically connecting your innermost self with the inner light of the crystal, linking yourself to the crystal's spirit. Keep breathing and

contemplate this idea. Listen to what your crystal is saying, be aware of your feelings, notice any images in your mind, and be mindful of any scents and tastes in the air. All the time, bathing in the aqua aura blueness that surrounds and fills you…

6 Stay in this place for at least 5–10 minutes, or much longer if you like, as there is much to be discovered here.

7 When you feel it is time to leave, thank the blue luminous spirit of the crystal for helping you and slowly make your way through the translucent blue world inside toward the door you came through.

8 Step out through the door and look up at the giant blue crystal in front of you. Feel yourself starting to grow, getting bigger and bigger and bigger until you are sitting holding the crystal in your hand. Breathe, then gently open your eyes and see the aqua aura crystal in your hand.

Chapter Four

THE HUMAN ENERGY SYSTEM

The human energy system connects your inner being to the outside world around you. That is everything outside of your physical body. You sense things around you when you do not even realize that you are seeing, hearing, smelling, tasting, or touching anything. It is with these natural abilities that we can "hear" crystals with our very being. Understanding the human energy system takes you on another step to understanding crystal speak.

What Is the Human Energy System?

Our energy system is just as important as our physical body and mental state for our overall health and well-being. Together we call these the bodymind, which is interlaced with moving, vibrant, and constantly changing energy. The bodymind is composed of energy hot spots, or vortexes, called chakras (see page 77); the aura, an energy field around the body (see below); and meridians, which are lines of energy that run throughout the body and carry energy in a comparable way to arteries and veins carrying blood (see page 83). You should not think of the chakras, aura, and meridians as separate since they form one complete system with your physical body. Energy flows from your physical body and mind, through your energy hot spots (chakras) into your aura, and beyond into the outside world. At the same time, energy flows in the opposite direction, from the outside world into your body.

We have all experienced this flow of energy, perhaps as a warmth in the belly when you are feeling physically focused, the sensation of closeness you have without physically touching a partner or lover, and the tingling sensation in your hands and fingers when you know something you are feeling is right for you. With a little practice, you can begin to feel and recognize what your energy system is trying to tell you.

AURA

The aura is the first line of defence in the body's energy system, just as the skin is for the body's immune system. When your aura is healthy and strong, you are more likely to stay well, avoid illness, attract friends, and develop healthy and happy relationships. It has several layers, which create a rough egg shape of energy around the body: the Physical Aura layer is closest to the body, then, moving outwards, the other layers are the Etheric Aura, Emotional Aura, Vital Aura, Astral Aura, Lower Mental Plane that holds everything together, and the Higher Mental Plane above the head which connects us to the universe.

The Physical Aura

This is the layer closest to the skin and it provides a physical connection where our body feels the energy within the aura. It is one of the thinnest layers, at no more than 1cm (just under ½in.) deep. It is very difficult to distinguish how energy feels here, but it can be experienced like a breeze gently playing with the hairs on your arm.

The Etheric Aura

This is the second layer, going out another 2–4cm (¾–1½in.) from the body beyond the Physical Aura. This is your protective aura, which prevents energy upsets in the outer aura manifesting as disease in the physical body. It is one of the easiest layers to sense with a pendulum or your hand. The Etheric Aura is also the first layer that people are aware of when they begin to see auras—always appearing as a gray or purple tint. Interestingly, some people say that if you have a purple aura, you are a spiritual person, while if it is gray, you are seriously ill and likely to die soon. When people talk about the color of the aura, they are really referring to the Vital Aura (see page 76). When I started seeing auras myself, I was not aware of this little detail, so I spent a couple of days believing that half the population of the world was very spiritual and the other half were about to die!

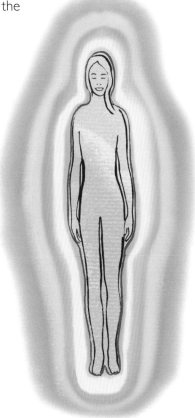

The Emotional Aura

Extending another 4–6cm (1½–2½in.), the Emotional Aura is, as the name suggests, the region where you hold emotional energy in your aura. Emotions attract similar emotions in both your life and your aura. So naturally happy people tend to attract other happy people into their life and sad people invite sad people. It can be helpful to think of the energy of emotions in your aura as like light and dark feelings. Light, happy emotions attract more of the same and create light, bright, happy, healthy areas in your aura, whereas dark areas of emotion attract darker areas of energy. Over time, these coalesce into dark, unhealthy, sad blobs of energy that draw energy from wherever they can, such as the other layers of your aura and your physical body—leaving you vulnerable to illness and disease—and from other people around you, which makes them feel that you are draining them. We have all experienced this at one time or another, that sense of discomfort around someone who you feel is draining you.

The Vital Aura

The Vital Aura is essential to health, with the energetic signatures of dis-ease appearing here well before any physical symptoms become apparent. Everything that has ever happened to you is recorded here and psychics who specialize in "aura readings" will look in this region to see into your past, present, and future. Unlike the other layers of the aura, which change little, the Vital Aura is in constant flux, changing color and size continuously, depending on your health, moods, and emotions. With a little practice you can learn to control this, expanding and contracting it at will and calming it when you are riled, so soothing the pain of emotional hurts.

The Astral Aura

Like the Vital Aura, the Astral Aura also freely changes shape and size, as it is involved in out-of-body experiences and astral travel. It acts as a bridge between you and the Universe around you, and it is where you begin to sense your surroundings and realize they are external to you.

The Lower Mental Plane

The Lower Mental Plane can be pictured as a very thin membrane—less than 1mm thick—that surrounds you. It is the edge of the aura, the boundary of you. Small holes can develop in the Lower Mental Plane, allowing energy to seep out and generally making you feel lethargic and susceptible to minor illnesses. These can be healed by specific crystal-healing combing techniques working with a quartz crystal.

The Higher Mental Plane

The Higher Mental Plane is your connection to spirit. It hovers a few centimeters above the Lower Mental Plane. It is vulnerable to outside influences, such as a child being told to ignore their "imaginary friend," as if they didn't exist. But the more you use your connection to spirit, the stronger it becomes. When this has become normal for you, again you will experience the guiding hand of the Universe all around you.

Chakras and Meridians

Chakra is a Sanskrit word meaning "wheel". They are called this because people who see energy see swirling balls of energy which are often represented as wheels or disks in two-dimensional illustrations. Chakras are the areas within the body where there is most energy because they appear where the meridians, or energy channels, cross or bulge together. These energy hot spots are the easiest places to exchange energy with the outside world. They expand beyond your physical body into the aura, which allows them to function as perfect conduits for energy to flow between the physical body and the aura. Although there are hundreds of minor chakras, we focus in this book on the seven major chakra system that is most followed in the West.

For each chakra described below, I also suggest a couple of crystals that resonate well with that chakra, as well as its exact location, color, and fragrance associations. You will find that many more crystals work well with each chakra and these are given in the Crystal Finder (see pages 102–39).

CROWN CHAKRA
on the top of the head.

BROW CHAKRA
(also known as the third eye chakra)—in the center of the forehead, above the eyebrows.

THROAT CHAKRA
in the center of the throat.

HEART CHAKRA
in the center of the chest.

SOLAR PLEXUS CHAKRA
behind the soft cartilage at the bottom of the breast bone.

SACRAL CHAKRA
just below your belly button. Try placing your thumb on your belly button with your palm on your belly—your sacral chakra will be under the palm of your hand.

BASE CHAKRA
at the coccyx at the base of the spine.

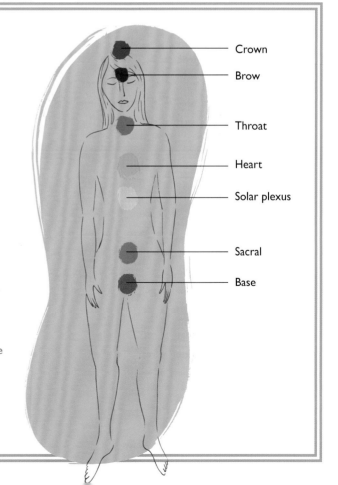

Crown

Brow

Throat

Heart

Solar plexus

Sacral

Base

Base Chakra

Location: Coccyx, base of the spine

Crystal: Red jasper, hematite

Color: Red

Fragrance: Patchouli

The base chakra, also known as the first chakra, is found at the base of the spine. It focuses on survival, supporting strength, determination, and everything we find nurturing, such as our friends and family or nature. It is regarded in Hindu traditions as the place where the resting kundalini is stored (this is a form of divine feminine energy in Hinduism). It is the energy hot spot that connects us to the Earth and the earth plane while we are living this life. A healthy base chakra will keep you grounded, and it is the driving force that helps you move forward in life.

Keywords: Advancing in life, movement, freedom, release, letting go, death, change, new beginnings, grounding, new projects, abundance on a deep soul level, sensitive feelings and happy emotions, fulfillment, stress relief, calming, connection to the earth plane, nurture, mental peace and stability, being present in the moment, security, strength, confidence

Sacral Chakra

Location: Just below the belly button

Crystal: Carnelian, orange calcite

Color: Orange

Fragrance: Ylang ylang

The sacral chakra, also known as the second chakra, is located just below the navel. It is the center of creativity, desire, sexual emotion, and sexuality. It stimulates the creative life force that is needed to exist in the physical world. Some mystical traditions believe that this force is the basis for life itself. This is where we store good, healthy energy for future use.

Keywords: A store of instantly useable energy, energy on demand, inner strength, creativity, personal warmth, a "warm person," radiating energy, physical attraction, new beginnings, relationships, friendships, opportunity, joy, happiness, fertility, behavior patterns and addictions, power, confidence, emotional control, natural cycles, innocence

CREATIVE LIFE FORCE

This is also known as Universal Life Force Energy. The Chinese call this *chi* (or *qi*), the Japanese *ki*, and it's known as *prana* in ayurveda and yogic tradition. It is literally the energy that creates and sustains life. Life without this creative life force just cannot exist. I'll call it *chi* for simplicity.

A tale of science

The world of science does not believe that chi exists, but not recognizing this energy source leaves it in a slight quandary. This is because the only biochemical reaction that takes place within cells in the human body which "produces" energy is when ATP (adenosine triphosphate) is converted to ADP (adenosine diphosphate) and energy. But this reaction only produces around 20 percent of the energy required for an adult human to exist and function! So where does the rest of the energy come from? I talk about this in several of my books and usually say something along the following lines:

"Like so many aspects of alternative healing, we don't have to understand the source of this energy supply to be able to observe its effects."

However, as more and more evidence of dark matter and dark energy is found by scientists, it may well be that science has "discovered" chi (see Dark Matter and Dark Energy box, page 64).

Solar Plexus Chakra

Location: Behind the soft cartilage at the bottom of the breastbone

Crystal: Citrine, tiger's eye

Color: Yellow

Fragrance: Neroli

The solar plexus chakra, also known as the third chakra, is found at the solar plexus—from where it gets its name—in the middle of the body below the breastbone. It is the center of personal power, ambition, desire, and emotion. Touch and feelings are processed through the solar plexus chakra, hence the phrase "gut feeling." It is the seat of our inner pendulum (see page 24). The solar plexus chakra is the physical center of the body, the point of "centering" where we come to stillness.

Keywords: Centering, protection, focus, ancient memory, balanced yin/yang, versatility, stress (especially 21st-century stress—see page 118, under rhodochrosite), belief, practical application of ideas, trust, honor, energy, flow, leadership, bravery, confidence, strength, logic, responsibility, self-esteem, acting on emotions

SOLAR PLEXUS CHAKRA: A SOURCE OF VERSATILITY

There is an old adage that stress goes to the weakest part of the body. This is considered true and, as a result, imbalance in the solar plexus chakra can show as almost any physical, emotional, psychological, or spiritual symptom throughout the body or its energy system. A healthy third chakra promotes versatility, as you learn to adapt from one situation to the next.

Heart Chakra

Location: Center of the chest

Crystal: Malachite, ruby

Color: Green

Fragrance: Rose

Located in the center of the chest, and sometimes called the fourth chakra, this is the center of love and compassion. It relates to your connection with everyone and everything around you. Spirituality, in the sense of "a connection to everything," is a key concept of love. Without this connection we are unable to share the love we all have inside us.

Keywords: Love, spiritual love, relationships, connection, inner truth, soul, spirit, emotional energy, moving forward on our life path, hope, sparkling energy, love of life, empathy, fearlessness, sharing, animals, harmony, kindness, gentleness, peace

HEART CHAKRA: MAKING CONNECTIONS

This energy hot spot is the deepest point inside us, where the outside world meets our inner being. With each breath we take, we inhale part of the outside world and exchange energy with it (through the physical process of gaseous exchange in the lungs). With this comes an awareness of our environment and a connection to it. We also share our own internal energy with the space and people around us as we exhale. This connection is the motor that sends love through the energy system, resulting, for example, in a bridge between the analytical mind and the feeling heart.

Throat Chakra

Location: Center bottom of the throat

Crystal: Turquoise, kyanite

Color: Blue

Fragrance: Lavender

The throat chakra, which is also known as the fifth chakra, is located at the bottom of the throat, in the middle of the neck above the collar bone. It is the center of communication and creative expression, relating to all forms of communication, such as speech, body language, and telepathy. It's the energy hot spot that tells the world how we are feeling and allows us to "talk our talk"—to express and explain our beliefs and points of view and to share the teaching we each have to give.

Keywords: Expression, communication, concentration, relaxation, emotional expression, self-expression, calmness, prayer, communication with spirit, ideals, justice, sacred knowledge, wisdom, advancement, career and employment prospects, leadership, marriage and partnerships, teaching children, childhood issues, confidence, mirror, freedom

Brow Chakra

Location: Center of forehead, above eyebrows

Crystal: Lapis lazuli, tanzanite

Color: Indigo

Fragrance: Sandalwood

The brow chakra is known as both the sixth chakra and the third eye. Located in the middle of the forehead above the eyebrows, it is the center of intuition, intellect, personal magnetism, and light. This is where creativity and inspiration combine. It helps with intuition, focuses psychic abilities, and stimulates wisdom.

Keywords: Mental balance and focus, creativity, clarity, thoughts, awareness, understanding our senses, extrasensory perception (ESP), intellect, innovation, ideas, creativity, inspiration, psychic abilities, information antenna, subconscious mind, learning, teaching, dreams, goals, ideals, and the door to possibility

Crown Chakra

Location: Top of the head

Crystal: Amethyst, labradorite

Color: Violet

Fragrance: Frankincense

Located at the top of the head and also known as the seventh chakra, the crown chakra is the center of spirituality, enlightenment, and dynamic thought. It facilitates the flow of wisdom to you from the Universe and connects you to the cosmic consciousness of all that is.

Keywords: Truth, illusion, ideals, self-awareness, balance, spirituality in the everyday physical world, connection, focus, purpose, direction, oneness, the big picture, flow, optimism, enthusiasm, uniqueness, originality, holistic, understanding

MERIDIANS

There are hundreds of lines of energy flowing through the body, and these are known as meridians, or in some yogic traditions, as nadis. They facilitate the flow of energy in the same way that your arteries and veins carry blood to where it is needed. Meridians create chakras, or energy hot spots, where they meet because the energy is more concentrated there. The chakras carry this energy back and forth to the aura, thus completing the energy system of many living things, from insects to humans in the evolutionary range.

exercises: WITH ENERGY

Here are two practical exercises that you can try with a partner or friend. The first to sense and experience the energy of the aura and the second the energy of the chakras. With both of these exercises take your time; the slower you do them the more you will feel.

Exercise 1

1 Sit facing your partner, so you are about 60cm (2ft) apart.
2 Hold out your hands, with palms facing your partner, and very slowly move your hands toward theirs—they should hold out their hands in the same way. You will start to feel their energy as a pressure building. The energy will become stronger the nearer both your hands get, until you reach a point where your hands are close together, but not touching—this is where the energy will be strongest.
3 If you slowly go past this optimal point, closer to your partner's hands, then the energy or pressure drops off. If you keep going until your hands touch, you will notice that it does not seem as powerful as when they were slightly apart. However, if you maintain the physical contact, the energy will start to build again.

Exercise 2

1 This time, one of you should lie down on their back, so the other person can use a flat palm to sense the energy in their partner's body.

2 Move your hand very slowly, from your partner's feet up to their crown chakra, about 5cm (2in.) above the body. See what you feel. You are looking for differences in energy, different feelings. It is easiest to sense this at the chakras, which are the body's energy hot spots, or at any areas of injury or disease. Your hand may feel hotter or cooler, or tingly like pins and needles, or there may even be a change in pressure, as if your hand is being drawn toward their body or pushed away. The slower you move your hand, the easier it is and the more you will feel.

3 When you have finished, swap over so your partner can feel your energy hot spots too.

exercise:
FEELING AND SENSING CRYSTALS WITH YOUR CHAKRAS

Another way of sensing crystal energy is to sense the reactions of your chakras. You might want to create a relaxing space for this exercise, with a comfortable bed, cushions, or therapy bed to lie on, dimmed light or candlelight, and some gentle, relaxing, or inspiring music.

1 Choose a selection of seven crystals—it doesn't really matter which crystals you work with, as long as they are all different.
2 Lie on your back and place one crystal on your base chakra. Then close your eyes for a couple of minutes and see how it feels and what you are aware of. You may want to record your thoughts and feelings as you go along.
3 Move the crystal to the sacral chakra and close your eyes. Again, record your feelings. Then place this first crystal on the chakra—the base chakra or sacral chakra—where you felt it most strongly.
4 Take the next crystal and repeat this process for the remaining six chakras. As you work through all the crystals, you will discover that you need less time with them on a chakra before you start to become aware of it. Place the seventh crystal on the empty chakra.
5 When you have placed the seven crystals, close your eyes and just bathe in the gentle crystal energy, enjoying a lovely, relaxing crystal-healing self-treatment.

The most interesting observation for me is that once you get into the flow of this exercise, you become aware of which chakras will respond most to a crystal before you've even placed it on your body. It's as if the crystals are talking to your chakras—which, of course, they are! Your chakras are starting to translate crystal speak (see page 45) for you into chakra energy that you can understand.

   If you are working with clients, you will become increasingly aware of where crystals need to go on them without having to ask your pendulum, but you can always check back with this whenever you are in doubt.

Using Chakras as Aids for Diagnosis

There are practical methods you can turn to for interpreting the messages from your crystals, using the body as a translator. Whether you are working on yourself or a client, the chakras can help to interpret the messages of the crystals. For example, if you are selecting crystals for a client and turquoise comes up for the base chakra, this could imply that they are having difficulty communicating or explaining their next step to another or others. You will discover there are countless possibilities when you combine the interpretation of chakras in this chapter with the information in the Crystal Finder (see pages 102–39).

FEELING AND SENSING CRYSTALS WITH YOUR AURA

Another practical way of experiencing crystal energies, and other energies for that matter, is with your aura. A lovely exercise is to create a circle of one type of crystal that's large enough for you to sit or lie inside. Ideally, the crystals should all be touching, but don't worry if you haven't got enough of the same type of crystal to do this—just have at least four crystals around you and create an approximate circle.

Close your eyes and sit quietly in the crystal circle for at least two minutes; you can sit for much longer if you wish. Be aware of which crystals are speaking to you in the circle around you, or, if you are not sure exactly which, then notice the direction they are in. Sometimes you will experience an overall feeling while in the circle. Repeat this exercise with as many different types of crystal as you have.

Setting up a number of crystal circles and then spending a few minutes in each one can be an amazing way of realizing that not all crystals of the same type have the same message for you. This is also a fun exercise to do with friends, with each of you spending a few minutes in a crystal circle before you all change places and sit in another circle. Do this until everyone has experienced each of the circles you set up.

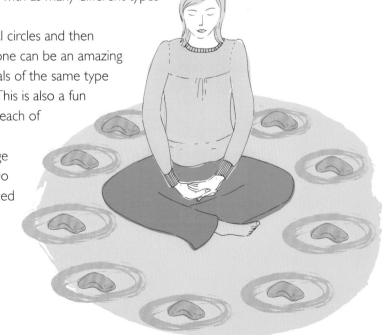

meditation:
CONNECT WITH YOUR CHAKRAS

This meditation will help you connect your chakras with crystal power. You will need seven crystals, one for each chakra. Work with the ones suggested with each of the chakras in this chapter, any that you have in your collection from the Crystal Finder on pages 102–39, or even crystals you feel resonate with each of your chakras (they don't have to match the chakra colors).

1 Lie down on your back and do the Meditation Preparation that you learned at the start of the book (see page 18).
2 Now place the seven crystals you have chosen on their relevant chakra. It is easier to start at the base chakra and work up. You can place the crown chakra crystal on a pillow on the floor or in bed, just above your head. Close your eyes.
3 Imagine there is a bright red light below your feet in the earth. As you breathe in, imagine that the bright red light is rising through your feet, into your legs, and up to the base chakra at the bottom of your spine. Let the bright red light surround the crystal on your base chakra. How does this feel? Stay with this feeling for two minutes. It is all right if the feeling changes, but keep your focus on the crystal on your base chakra.

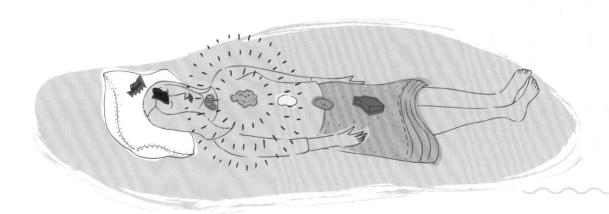

CRYSTALS AND CHAKRA BALANCE

Your chakras go in and out of balance all day as they react to events and different energies that you encounter during the day. This is natural and healthy. Sometimes one or more chakra goes a significant way out of balance and takes a long time, or needs help, to find equilibrium.

Connecting your chakras to crystals is a tried-and-tested way of both understanding these crystals and balancing your chakras. It's a daily exercise to keep you healthy.

4 Allow the bright red light to change into a bright orange light as it flows up to your sacral chakra. Check how this feels for you as the bright orange light engulfs the crystal on your sacral chakra. Spend two minutes here focused on the crystal bathing in the bright orange light on your sacral chakra.

5 Repeat this process as the light keeps moving up your body, spending two minutes at each chakra, with the bright colors changing to yellow at the solar plexus, green at the heart, light blue by the throat, indigo on the brow, and violet at the crown chakra at the top of your head. Focus on the brightly colored light as it immerses the crystal on each chakra.

6 When you have finished working with the crown chakra crystal, imagine the violet color becoming a bright white light and rising up above your head. In your mind watch the light as it goes way, way up into the sky… When you feel ready, open your eyes.

Chapter Five

CRYSTAL DIVINATION

Crystals and divination have been employed by people since time immemorial, whether by the shaman or priest to translate the words of their gods and spirits or the private consultation about what your future holds or what to do about a specific situation. Here we will explore some of the history of divination and look forward to practical applications for you today, creating your own crystal divination basket and starting to use it in several different ways.

What is Divination?

Divination comes from the Latin *divinare*, meaning "to foresee, to foretell, to predict, to prophesy." It is implied that this is achieved through mysterious, magical, spiritual, or supernatural means. But no matter how divination is achieved, it is in essence contacting the divine in the search of answers—whatever you believe the divine to be.

We have been divining the future and contacting our divinities ever since we became sentient humans. Even the archeological site at Maropeng, near Pretoria, in South Africa—one of the earliest prehuman sites, located in the Cradle of Humankind—shows extensive evidence of crystals and stone technology (see page 14). Archeological evidence also suggests the early practice of divination, using bones and stones as a toolkit, to see into the future.

Carnelian beads

Human beings (that's us) only arrived on the scene around 300,000 years ago. One of the most renown human archeological sites is in Hadar, Ethiopia, where the skeleton of "Lucy" was found. The site was a small farming village and estimated to be about 200,000 years old. As well as several graves, with Lucy being the best-preserved skeleton, archeologists also found many astragali, which in this case are ankle bones from sheep. These exhibited different but constant markings on the six sides. Anthropologists believe these bones were used as dice in some unknown form of divination to seek the wisdom of gods or spirits. Astragali are still used today in a form of divination called Shagai in Mongolia, as well as in other countries in Central Asia. In every grave they also found carnelian beads, which were presumably used to protect the person's spirit on their journey into the afterlife.

Much, much later, classical Greek scholars, such as Socrates and Homer, talked of prophecy in a matter-of-fact way—it was very much a part of everyday life in ancient Greece. Indeed, the Sibyls (Greek prophetesses) at ancient holy sites were consulted as oracles by all levels of society. Quartz crystal balls were also worked with for scrying (a type of divination that involves gazing into a crystal object) as early as the 3rd century BCE in ancient Greece and possibly 2,000 years earlier in China. The origins of Western medicine are intertwined with Hellenic divination and the later Judeo-Christian Bible is also full of prophecies. There are 1,239 prophecies in the Old Testament and another 578 in the New Testament according to J. Barton Payne's *Encyclopaedia of Biblical Prophecy*.

Hippocrates created much of the theory on which modern medicine is based, and the Hippocratic oath has not changed in 2,500 years. His theories came from intertwining the spiritual with the physical, specifically the humors—blood, phlegm, yellow bile, and black bile—spiritual beliefs, and thoughts of the mind. It is thought that Socrates, who greatly influenced Hippocrates, first suggested that the mind, and thus belief, was the most important part of healing. The humors really took the place of previous spiritual beliefs whose treatment was guided by divination.

Tarot cards

In Africa, various tribes use divination baskets, containing crystals and stones as well as other meaningful objects. These baskets are still used by the Ndembu people of the Republic of Zambia, for example, to identify the causes of societal stress and to heal them. For instance, if someone steals food from another tribal member, they are not guilty of a crime. Instead, the rest of the tribe are guilty of allowing one of their members to be so hungry and desperate that they had to steal to feed their family. It is an interesting idea for any society.

WHY WORK WITH CRYSTALS TO FIND ANSWERS?

Today, crystals are worked with extensively in many forms of divination, sometimes to show answers to queries, other times to help the seer to see more clearly. They are linked to Tarot cards and various crystal oracle card packs. Overleaf you can find out how to make your own crystal divination basket.

exercise:

CREATE YOUR OWN CRYSTAL DIVINATION BASKET

To make a divination basket, you can work with any number of crystals, but I suggest starting with 12 crystals or tumble polished stones. The more you have to choose from, the better. You'll also need a wicker basket, wooden bowl, or large pouch made from a natural, hard-wearing material like leather or cotton denim (I would advise against using ceramic bowls, as they can be noisy, or a thin cotton or silk pouch that can be easily torn by the crystals).

You Will Need

12 crystals or tumble polished stones, about 2–4cm (¾–1½in.) in size
Crystal pendulum (see page 23)
Pen and notepad (or an electronic device such as a laptop or tablet)
Wicker basket, wooden bowl, or large pouch

1   Find a quiet space where you will not be disturbed.
2   Choose six crystals from the selection you have available. Do this in whatever way works for you and remember you can always turn to your crystal pendulum for help.
3   Pick one of the six crystals and put the others to the side for the time being. We will come back to these later.
4   For the best results, take your time and don't rush the process. Hold the crystal in your right hand. Notice how it feels and how it makes you feel. Now hold it in your left hand. Check how your left hand feels or if the crystal makes you feel different now it is in your left hand compared to when it was in your right hand. Also be aware of how your right hand feels now it is no longer holding the crystal.
5   Explore your feelings inside your body. What do you notice? Any colors? Sit quietly with the crystal in whichever hand you prefer and see what it has to say to you. Perhaps a word? An idea? A whole book! Or a picture or shape inside the crystal or in your mind? Maybe it is a feeling somewhere inside you or an emotion rising or sinking in your body? Do you feel happy or sad? Record your experience. Write down

as many keywords as you can—you can always expand on these and add more in-depth sections later.

6 Repeat steps 3 to 5 with each of the five remaining crystals.

7 Once you have finished with all six crystals, and recorded your experiences and feelings, put them to one side. Again, we will return to these later.

8 Now write down six headings (topics or people) that are important to you, such as Love, Family, Work/Career, Partner/Spouse, and so on, across the top of a page. Then write how you feel about each of these six topics below the six headings. This can be as detailed as you like—in fact, the more details you have, the better it will be in the long run. But focus on getting as many keywords as you can in the first instance and expand their meaning or add more information later.

9 When you have written as much as you feel is necessary, carefully choose one crystal from the selection you have left to represent each of your six headings. This needs to be a crystal that resonates with the topic or person for you. It doesn't matter why: it can be any reason or feeling you notice such as how it feels, its color, or the crystal's healing attributes, for example. Check the Crystal Finder (see pages 102–39) for more ideas. You can also ask your crystal pendulum for help here if you need to. Record this information.

10 You have now chosen six more crystals to add to the first group of six, giving you a total of 12 crystals to work with. The first six crystals have told you what they want to represent. We will call this Group A. You then picked the second six crystals and essentially told them what they will represent for you. This is Group B.

Perform a Crystal Reading

For the next part of the exercise you will need a friend to practice on.

1   Start by asking your friend to select one crystal from both Group A and B. Now you can translate the meaning the crystals have expressed to you for them. Some keywords will seem more important than others and this will change each time you do a crystal reading. You might feel this, or they might seem brighter on the page. You may even feel as if you are being guided. Remember, you can always rely on your crystal pendulum for help if you need it. Then ask your friend how relevant the information is.

2   In the first part of the exercise you divined six crystals and then six more, and you know what each represents. Your friend has now chosen two crystals, one of which has communicated its meaning to you and the other you have given a meaning to. So, in effect you have given your friend a crystal reading—you have divined their future.

3   As you gain more experience with this, you can ask your friend to select any number of crystals they are drawn to from Group A and/or B.

4   The initial 12 crystals are just a starting point. You can, of course, keep using the system as it is with these crystals, or you can add more whenever you feel the need for an extra topic, as for your second set of six crystals, or you are intuitively drawn to add a crystal to your system, just as you were for your first set of six crystals.

5   Over time, you may end up with hundreds of crystals in your crystal divination basket or, of course, you can stick with the original 12 crystals.

Crystal Casting

There is another method of crystal divination, and this is my favorite. It uses a similar method to that employed by the Ndembu people and their divination basket (see page 93). To begin with, you can work with the 12 crystals you have already selected in the first part of the exercise and you'll need to remember what each crystal represents. Although you don't have to know the names of every crystal at this point, it's nice if you do. You'll also need your own divination basket and a large, flat area.

Rose quartz

1　Place the divination basket filled with your crystals in front of you and still yourself with your Meditation Preparation (see page 18).

2　When you feel ready, gently throw all the crystals out of the basket in front of you. This is called casting. If you are using a table, make sure none of the crystals fall off.

3　First, look for overall patterns or shapes, as this can sometimes give the essence or direction of the reading. For example, a general shape resembling a butterfly would suggest the reading is all about change, whereas an arrow may suggest the order in which the crystals should be read—that is, toward the apex.

4.　Next, look for small groups of crystals. For instance, if you see one crystal representing love standing out for you, look at the others nearby and see if you can interpret this small grouping as relating to love.

5　To help you learn, photograph your crystal cast with a camera or your smartphone, label the crystals on the picture, and annotate these labels with your interpretaion to keep a record of your results. You will be surprised how many times the same or similar shapes appear!

6　You can keep doing these readings for more and more people. As you do, you will discover that each crystal retains its original meaning.

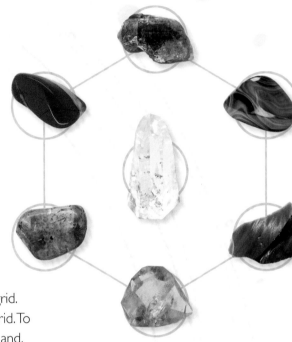

exercise:
CREATE A CRYSTAL GRID TO SUPPORT DIVINATION

You can create a healing crystal grid for yourself, or to speed up the outcome of a reading for yourself or someone else.

You Will Need

Your crystal divination set (see page 94)
Your quartz master crystal (see page 36)

1 Select one crystal from the second group of crystals (this is Group B) that best represents the topic or issue at the center of the reading. Focus your intent on this crystal or what it represents throughout this process.

2 Then arrange six crystals from your first group of crystals (Group A) around this central crystal in a hexagonal shape. The hexagon represents the six sides of a quartz crystal and will add focus to the crystal grid.

3 Now you need to activate the crystal grid. To do this, take your quartz master crystal and, holding it about 3–5cm (1¼–2in.) above the crystal grid, with the termination pointing downward, move it clockwise over each of the outer crystals six times. You should move around the crystals in the grid in a clockwise direction too. As you move over each crystal, think of its meaning for you and how this might relate to the central crystal. If you are not sure of this, just accept that it is part of the equation of fulfillment. Finally, activate the central crystal in the same way, moving clockwise six times.

4 Once you have finished, leave the grid in place for a factor of six. This can be minutes, hours, days, or weeks, depending on circumstances, such

as the availability of crystals and space. When I'm with a client, I am always happy to work through the process during the session and then remove the grid afterward. They often take the crystals home, so they can recreate the grid for themselves and activate it daily at home over the longer term.

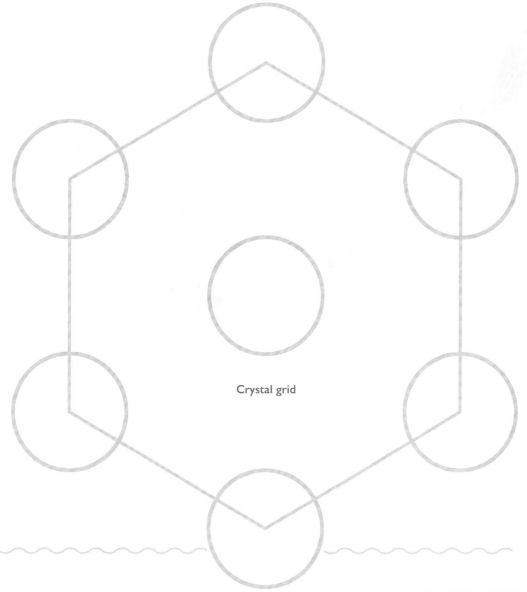

Crystal grid

exercise:
TREATMENTS WITH YOUR DIVINATION CRYSTALS

This simple treatment involving the laying on of stones can be highly beneficial for the recipient after a crystal divination reading (whether this is for a client or friend or family member). The crystals are directly linked to any issues whether physical, emotional, mental, or spiritual that the client/ friend may have. It is the same as having preselected crystals for a client because you know they are the correct ones to help the presented symptoms. You will need your quartz master crystal and seven crystals from your selection of divination crystals, one for each chakra (see pages 77–83). You can choose from the 12 crystals you started with in Groups A and B (see page 94), but also from any others you have added since.

1　Focus on each chakra, one at a time, as you select its crystal. You can do this intuitively or ask your crystal pendulum to help you choose. In this instance, it doesn't matter which groups the crystals come from.
2　Then lay each selected crystal on its relevant chakra.
3　Take your quartz master crystal and, holding it about 3cm (1¼ in.) above the crystal on the base chakra, with the termination pointing down, move it in a clockwise direction for 1–2 minutes, to activate the crystal. As you do this, think about the crystal, what it means for you in your divination system, and how it may be relevant to the chakra on which it's placed.

4 Repeat this for each of the remaining crystals and chakras, moving up the body toward the crown chakra.

5 Leave the crystals in place for 5–10 minutes, so the recipient can bathe completely in the crystal energy and receive the fullest benefit from the treatment.

6 Remove the crystals one by one, starting at the crown chakra and working your way down the body to the base chakra.

7 If you have a selenite aura wand, you might like to brush down and then seal the recipient's aura.

Selenite aura wand

CRYSTAL DIVINATION MEDITATIONS

Practice this meditation to help you gain a deeper insight into the meaning of each of your crystals in your crystal divination basket. Place your 12 crystals on a table in front of you. (You can do this with as many crystals as you collect in your crystal divination basket.) Practice your Meditation Preparation (see page 18).

Open your eyes and look at your 12 crystals in front of you. Let your eyes fall into soft focus, you can do this by focussing just past them. Allow yourself to become aware of one crystal that stands out for you. This might be one that draws your focus and appears clearer, or one that looks brighter as if it has a glowing aura around it, whichever it is, is calling you. Without moving any crystals focus on this one. As you are looking at it be aware of any other crystals that are glowing or coming into focus or attracting your attention in any way. These crystals are talking to the one you are focused on.

Think about what is happening in your own life and what you may need the crystals' help for. Then note the crystals that are chatting to you. Close your eyes and gently breathe for a minute or two. When you are ready open your eyes and bring your focus back into the room.

If you don't know what all the crystals mean for you, you can look up their meanings in the notes you made earlier in this chapter.

Chapter Six
THE CRYSTAL FINDER

The Right Crystal for You

This chapter is designed with three concepts in mind.

THE FIRST is to help you identify any crystals you may already have, as well as those you may come across. All the crystals in this directory are listed under their most commonly occurring and commercially available color to make it easy for you to find them. Refer to the pictures, descriptions, and color references throughout to guide you. Many of the crystals are also commonly available as tumble polished stones and cut and polished into many shapes such as spheres, standing points, hearts, and a vast variety of animals.

THE SECOND concept is to inspire you to make crystals your friends, so you can talk to them and see what they have to say. I want to help you see and hear their messages, and here, due to the inevitably limited space available in a book, I give you a brief introduction to a little of the wisdom the crystals have imparted to me. Take this information as a starting point, a stepping stone on your own crystal journey. For each crystal, I have also included common sources, their astrological and chakra associations, and their key healing attribute(s). If you would like further information on the healing benefits of crystals, I have written other books that you might find helpful, and some of these are listed on the back flap of the book.

THE THIRD concept behind this directory is that once you have created your own crystal divination basket (see page 94), it is intended as a guide to both selecting and interpreting the crystals in your set.

RED

Red jasper

Description: A variety of quartz colored red by iron oxide inclusions.

Common sources: Worldwide—especially India and Brazil

Astrological associations: Taurus, Aries

Chakra: Base

Healing: General tonic to help you keep well.

Crystal Connections

Keywords: Moving forward, keeping your feet on the ground

Crystal talk: Red jasper says to me that it is time for you to move forward in your life. But to do this you must shed the past. It can feel as if you're standing in the rain from a cloud burst and the water is washing everything you don't need into the ground. Then, when the time is right, you can take your next step forward. Red jasper doesn't want you to go spinning off in a dream world, but rather keep your feet firmly on the ground as you travel on your amazing path.

Ruby

Description: A red variety of corundum that forms hexagonal tabular crystals.

Common sources: India, Madagascar, Thailand, Myanmar

Astrological associations: Cancer, Leo, Scorpio, Sagittarius

Chakra: Heart

Healing: Promotes a healthy menstrual cycle, as well as immune and circulatory systems.

Crystal Connections

Keywords: Longevity, passion, love, fertility

Crystal talk: Ruby tells you to open your heart and release your passion. It shows you opportunities for new beginnings, whether in relationships or your career, and focuses your creative force. It tells you, and helps you, to feel the

connection between your head, your heart, and your feet and to act with passion whenever you need to. If anything is worth doing, put your whole being into it.

Brecciated jasper

Description: Formed as jasper is shattered by tectonic activity, such as earthquakes and eruptions, within the Earth. The spaces that are created in the damaged rock are then naturally filled with more jasper, chalcedony, and microcrystalline quartz. The deep red colors are due to hematite inclusions within the jasper.

Common sources: Worldwide—especially Australia, Brazil, Canada, Egypt, India, Madagascar, Russia, Republic of South Africa, USA, and Uruguay

Astrological associations: Aries, Taurus

Chakra: Base

Healing: Female reproductive system, including the womb, ovaries, fallopian tubes, fibroids, and general fertility

Crystal Connections

Keywords: Repair, putting things back together again, focus, points of view

Crystal talk: I have always wondered at this naturally broken and repaired variety of jasper. What happens when you're feeling broken, or it seems as if your whole world is falling apart? That's exactly what was happening to a client of mine. She was going through a divorce and hated living in the family home with an abusive husband, but her lawyers told her she had to stay. We found that brecciated jasper can be a good friend to have in your corner. For those times when your head is in a fog, it helps you to focus and perhaps see the different sides of a situation. It reminds you that no matter how bad things seem or how broken you feel, you can put it all back together again. It won't be the same, but there can be a more beautiful life just waiting for you to start living. We are made up of all the events that have ever happened in our life. Brecciated jasper can help you choose to reset them to give you a powerful inner strength.

Zircon

Description: Short, square prismatic crystals that can often be octahedral. Colors include red, colorless, brown, green, gray, or yellow.
Common sources: Worldwide—especially Australia, Brazil, India, Pakistan, and USA
Astrological associations: Leo, Virgo, Sagittarius
Chakra: Base
Healing: Aura, the past, past lives

Crystal Connections

Keywords: Self-esteem, self-value, self-worth
Crystal talk: Zircon is the oldest crystal on the planet. The younger ones are often two billion years old! Some of the oldest are 4.4 billion years old and they were the first crystals to form as the Earth developed its crust. With age comes wisdom. These crystals have seen everything you can imagine. I've found that they give my clients a calming energy when they start to worry or panic. It's as if you have a very tough and dependable friend on your side. Your friend wants to tell you to be brave and confident, and to let your light shine a clear path for yourself and others around you. People will be drawn to your light, as zircon tells you to switch on your personal magnetism and let your aura glow.

Garnet

Description: Forms dodecahedral and trapezohedral crystals and combinations, masses, and layered "plates." Colors include red, pink, melanite, orange, red/purple, and shades of green, yellow, and brown.
Common sources: India, Russia, USA
Astrological associations: Leo, Virgo, Capricorn, Aquarius
Chakra: Heart
Healing: Blood and circulatory system

Crystal Connections

Keywords: Courage, flow, vitality, abundance, change, creative energy
Crystal talk: I've noticed in the crystal showroom that on

the rare occasion a customer comes in feeling a bit down, holding a garnet crystal can almost instantly lift them up. If you're having an emotional wobble, it will act as a keel, bringing stability to your ship. It will remind you that you are naturally aware, even psychic, and that you can see what is coming if you would just stop and listen. It reminds us that sometimes we just need to breathe. Garnet will help you plot a smoother course as you sail through the chaos and storms that life can throw at you. It will tell you to pause, so you can see the magic unfold around you, and to focus on your spiritual belief, even if it is different from that of everyone around you.

Red calcite

Description: A red variety of calcite commonly formed in masses.
Common source: Mexico
Astrological association: Cancer
Chakra: Base
Healing: Calms physical energy, good for ADHD (attention deficit hyperactivity disorder), panic attacks, and OCD (obsessive compulsive disorder).

Crystal Connections

Keywords: Grounding, stills a manic mind
Crystal talk: Whenever I feel that I am trying to do too much and be in too many places in too little time, and I'm suffering from 21st-century stress, red calcite is my go-to crystal. It tells me that I am running around chasing my own tail and it is now time to chill…I need to slow down physically, emotionally, and mentally. Stop piling pressure on yourself. Many of the things you think you must do, you don't. So, whatever is causing you stress, it is time to take a red calcite chill-out.

ORANGE

Carnelian

Description: An orange variety of chalcedony in the form of pebbles. Colors may tint toward red, pink, or brown.
Common sources: Brazil, India, Uruguay
Astrological associations: Taurus, Cancer, Leo
Chakra: Sacral
Healing: Energy, immune system (especially defence against viruses), digestion

Crystal Connections

Keywords: Feel better, inspiration, vitality
Crystal talk: Carnelian supports my positivity in so many ways—positive health, positive mental attitude, self-worth, self-esteem, compassion, confidence, and personal power. Carnelian reminds you to just get out there and do it and not to hold back, whether this concerns your home or career, relationships, or business. It says it will help you clear your mind, focus your intent, inspire you, help you find answers in your past, and give you the courage and strength you need to achieve. Carnelian tells you that you can break barriers: both the ones other people and society create and those you put in your own way. It will help you understand how you feel and why you deserve what you receive.

Orange calcite

Description: A bright to pale orange variety of calcite masses.
Common source: Mexico
Astrological associations: Cancer, Leo
Chakra: Sacral
Healing: Promotes happiness—after all, they say laughter is the best medicine.

Crystal Connections

Keywords: Happiness, vitality
Crystal talk: One day, I was teaching a crystal healing class and knew one of the students needed orange

calcite in their life. I didn't know why, but the crystal was looking at her and glowing every time she walked past. I placed the orange calcite in her hand and she smiled instantly, her face quickly producing a broad smile which morphed into raucous laughter! Orange calcite brings such happiness and joy. When you hold orange calcite and you need to hear its message, it can feel as if it will make you laugh and smile. It helps you see the funny side of most things, release any anger and aggression, balance your energy, and bring calmness to your mind and body. This can help you to relax, even in the most stressful of situations. It also has a knack of steering you away from dangers to your health.

Vortex healing crystal

Description: A variety of quartz crystal with surface hematite deposits that create an orange or red color.
Only source: Sedona (Arizona, USA)
Astrological associations: Aries, Leo
Chakra: Sacral, brow
Healing: Self-healing, wounds, pain relief

Crystal Connections

Keywords: Creativity, connection, expression
Crystal talk: I find vortex healing crystals are very powerful arbiters of change. They are perfect when you're feeling sorry for yourself. Any separation issues, whether divorce or death, a change of job or traveling far from family and friends, can bring feelings of anger, guilt, grief, loss, and sadness, as well as mood swings, depression, anxiety, panic attacks, and worry. This crystal offers support, so you can find the strength to communicate, which sometimes lets you avoid these feelings or helps to alleviate them. Vortex healing crystal is reminding you to tune in to your spirit guides and discover your creative side. It will help you find and follow your path to happiness.

Sunstone

Description: A type of oligoclase, which is a variety of the feldspar mineral plagioclase. Common inclusions of goethite and hematite are found in sunstone and give it its sparkle. Usually orange, but also yellow, red, green, blue, brown, colorless, and with copper schiller (adularescence).
Common sources: India, Norway, Sweden, USA, Australia
Astrological associations: Leo, Libra
Chakra: Crown
Healing: Vitality, longevity, skeletal issues

Crystal Connections

Keywords: Abundance, structure
Crystal talk: Sunstone talks of passion, vibrancy, craziness, beauty, and energy. I find it brings strength and shape to your dreams, creating the potential for realization. It helps you to let go of the fear of stress. This is different from the stress itself, as sunstone focuses on the dread, worry, and even panic that the thought of stress can create in the unsuspecting. Sunstone offers protection from those who want you to fail and whispers fabulously positive affirmations in your ear, giving you the power to deal with problems they put in your way.

YELLOW

Golden healer quartz

Description: A variety of quartz with an iron coating either on, or included within, the crystal, creating a pale golden yellow color.
Common sources: Worldwide—especially Brazil, China, Colombia, Madagascar, Russia, Republic of South Africa, USA (Arkansas)
Astrological associations: All
Chakra: All, especially heart
Healing: Supports all physical healing and the immune system, fights skin damage.

Crystal Connections

Keywords: Self-healing, leading to rebirth
Crystal talk: I came across golden healer quartz early in my crystal journey. One day, soon after I discovered it, a client who was going through a difficult divorce came to see me. She couldn't get the divorce out of her mind and it was starting to affect everything she did. She was lying on my therapy bed for a treatment and, as she closed her eyes, my new golden healer quartz crystal lit up as if to say: "My turn!" This crystal just wants you to do two things: to let go and then start again. Crystals have this marvelous way of telling each of us what it is we need to do, and when, if we listen to them. Of all crystals, this is truest of golden healer quartz. It speaks of strengthening yourself—your physical body, mind, and emotions—and boosting your aura (see page 74) to protect yourself. It tells you to cut the ties still binding you to the past. Once you are ready, it will help you let

go of unhealthy blocks in your lifestyle and change behavior patterns. So, let go of fear, past hurts, self-judgmental thoughts, and any beliefs that you are "not worth it" or "not worthy of it." Then, once golden healer "phase one" is complete, you can start on "phase two" and attract abundance, love, prosperity, emotional balance, and self-esteem. Golden healer quartz's mantra is "Cleanse, clear, reboot." It talks of happiness as you walk your walk through life.

Golden calcite

Description: Bright, golden-colored rhombohedral crystals
Common source: China
Astrological associations: Cancer, Leo
Chakra: Solar plexus
Healing: Kidneys, liver, fights infection

Crystal Connections

Keyword: Positivity
Crystal talk: Golden calcite works amazingly well for those clients of mine who live in fear, regardless of the cause. It speaks soothing words to calm your nerves and brings feelings of security and safety. It gives you a safe space in your life to ditch any self-limiting beliefs and allow your creativity to flow. Be inspired to change you, your surroundings, and even the world because every change you make will affect those around you and the new people you are about to meet in your life.

Citrine

Description: A yellow, golden, or lemon variety of quartz—the color comes from heat from volcanic and other Earth activity.
Common sources: Brazil, Madagascar, Democratic Republic of Congo, Russia, Namibia, Republic of South Africa, Republic of Zambia
Astrological associations: Aries, Gemini, Leo, Libra
Chakra: Solar plexus
Healing: Digestive system and wounds—whether you have a bruise or are recovering from major surgery, the physical wound will heal more quickly.

Crystal Connections

Keywords: Abundance, happiness
Crystal talk: Citrine is my go-to crystal whenever I need to make things happen. I wear it, carry it with me, have it on my desk, in my workshop room and therapy room at work, and in every room at home. It talks of new beginnings—whether in your personal life or career, citrine will lead you to new horizons that you can only dream of now. Citrine is known as the "money stone" and is renowned for attracting wealth, but the manner in which it does this makes it so much more valuable. It will whisper in your ear when you are trying to make a decision, help you learn, study, and digest new ideas, guide you in solving a problem, or inspire you when you need a creative spark. It always carries feelings of joy and happiness, making you feel better, whatever the situation you find yourself in.

Amber

Description: Fossilized resin from prehistoric trees that may have inclusions of ancient animal and/or plant material. Colors include yellow, orange, brown, blue, and green (artificial).
Common sources: Baltic Sea area; Latvia, Lithuania, Poland, Dominican Republic (blue)
Astrological associations: Leo, Aquarius
Chakra: Solar plexus
Healing: Detoxing, bacterial infections, traditionally employed as an antiseptic.

Crystal Connections

Keyword: Memories
Crystal talk: Amber talks of the past and what we can learn from our history. It always has a tale to tell. When I first worked with amber about 30 years ago, it felt light and brought a lightness to things. A feeling of clarity, cleansing, and purity. However, I was working with an older gentleman whose memory was starting to fade on a completely different issue. I added amber to the treatment to help him release some old trauma from the war. The next morning, I received a phone call from his daughter, asking me what I had done, as his memory was back to the sharpness it used to be years ago! Amber tells us to let it go. Whether your problem is physical, emotional, or mental, release the trapped energy and free your past.

Copper

Description: A metal occurring in free-form shapes, dendrites, plates, and, rarely, rhombohedral crystals.
Common sources: Australia, Canada, China, Chile, Democratic Republic of Congo, Mexico, Peru, Russia, USA, Zambia
Astrological associations: Taurus, Sagittarius
Chakra: Sacral
Healing: Joints, arthritis, tiredness

Crystal Connections

Keywords: Stimulates and balances the flow of energy
Crystal talk: Copper's message is that when you've given all you have to give, there is still a little bit more. It can help you get the tough things you have to do done. I find it is the right crystal when I need an extra little boost, as it seems to know what is required to help me push through my own barriers. It talks of fitness, wanting you to be as healthy as possible. Detox your body, let go of emotions, and be ready for new opportunities that will come your way.

Imperial topaz

Description: Golden prismatic crystals and alluvial pebbles
Common sources: Brazil, USA
Astrological associations: Leo, Sagittarius, Pisces
Chakra: Solar plexus, crown
Healing: Hormones, liver, 21st-century stress

Crystal Connections

Keyword: Connection
Crystal talk: I have always felt that imperial topaz wants to connect things such as people, energies, thoughts, and ideas—over any distance, near or far. For example, it helps me tune in to my other crystals when I don't have them at hand, perhaps when I'm at work and need something at home, or those in my crystal showroom when I'm traveling. All these connections are amplified by imperial topaz. Interestingly, it is the crystal that the

Mayans linked to Kinich Ahau, the god of the sun. For the Mayans, this god is responsible for the vastness of the four directions—north, west, south, east—and in the Universe and for connecting them. Imperial topaz reminds you to stop and breathe and helps you to meditate and to connect to everything you can imagine. It can bring a feeling of oneness.

Yellow fluorite

Description: Yellow cubic, octahedral, and rhombododecahedral crystals and masses
Common sources: China, UK
Astrological association: Leo
Chakra: Sacral
Healing: Cholesterol, liver, detoxing, weight loss

Crystal Connections

Keywords: Imagination, creativity
Crystal talk: Many years ago, someone gifted me a yellow fluorite crystal. At first, I noticed that my visions became more vivid and then my thoughts created clearer pictures in my mind. Like most fluorites, the yellow variety focuses the mind, but it also has the effect of balancing the right and left hemispheres of the brain. The left side tends to guide consciousness, thoughts, and decision-making, while the right concentrates more on creativity, ideas, and intuition. Yellow fluorite is telling you to put your ideas into action. I find it helpful for many of my clients and for those blocked by a mental trauma in particular.

Tiger's eye

Description: Created as quartz safely replaces asbestos, retaining its fibrous structure and producing an optical effect known as chatoyancy (a reflectance effect). Colors include gold, yellow, brown, blue, and red.
Common source: Republic of South Africa
Astrological association: Capricorn
Chakra: Solar plexus
Healing: Eyes, digestion and the digestive system

Crystal Connections

Keywords: Courage, strength
Crystal talk: Whenever I have a client who needs courage for any reason, such as speaking out or taking positive action, I always turn to tiger's eye to give them the inner strength to succeed. It promotes the courage you need to take actions. It doesn't matter if you are speaking out against a wrong or speaking in public to share your passion, tiger's eye will be a friend by your side or in your pocket. The message from tiger's eye is to trust your intuition. It opens the mind, creating possibilities and new openings.

GREEN

Jade

Description: Found as masses in many colors, including green, orange, brown, blue, cream, white, lavender, red, gray, and black. True jade includes jadeite and nephrite forms. Note that "new jade" is not jade, but a trade name for bowenite.
Common sources: Canada, China, Myanmar, USA
Astrological associations: Aries, Taurus, Gemini, Libra
Chakra: Heart
Healing: Skin, bones and joints, immune system, female reproductive system and menstrual cycles

Crystal Connections

Keywords: Wisdom, dreams, longevity
Crystal talk: Jade represents happiness, longevity, and wisdom; it is the perfect gift for a child. And it speaks of justice with the wisdom of the innocence of youth. Things are right or wrong, and no matter how convenient it might sometimes be, there is no wishy-washy, misconstrued middle ground where there are excuses for how we act. Jade calls on you to take responsibility for your actions and the words you say. Speak only kind words from your heart. If you don't have any kind words to say about someone, then be still. This is wise and makes for a happy life. Be with people who make you happy.

Aventurine

Description: A variety of quartz with mica inclusions, giving a speckled or sparkly appearance. Commonly green, but also found in other colors such as blue, brown, peach, red, and white.
Common sources: Brazil, India
Astrological association: Aries
Chakra: Heart
Healing: Muscles, nerves, reactions, heart, lungs, fights energy vampires.

Crystal Connections

Keywords: Calming, soothing, emotions
Crystal talk: Aventurine talks of patience and calm—taking your time to get things right and remaining relaxed, even if others are pushing you to go quicker than you feel comfortable with. It wants you to take deep breaths into your lungs and slow down. It also reminds you to find people on your wavelength and steer clear of those energy vampires who zap your energy. The sparkly mica inclusions help to reflect your soul.

Malachite

Description: Forms crystalline aggregates, druses, botryoidal structures, and clusters of radiating fibrous crystals. Green with various shades of green and black bands. Perfect single prismatic crystals are rare.
Common sources: Democratic Republic of Congo, USA
Astrological associations: Scorpio, Capricorn
Chakra: Heart
Healing: Heart, blood, immune system, inflammation, tissue regeneration, sleep

Crystal Connections

Keywords: Emotional baggage, emotional balance, detoxing
Crystal talk: Malachite says sleep. It reminds us that our body, mind, and soul all repair when we are sleeping and of the importance of having a good night's sleep. It is not about slowing down at all; it is a

directive to do everything at 100 percent—including sleeping. And it does not pull any punches. In fact, it can be like a sledgehammer for emotions, smashing the ones that are unhelpful out of the park! At the same time, it is also super nurturing for those useful emotions you are experiencing. Malachite will also help you interpret your dreams and turn them into reality.

Unakite

Description: A mixture of green epidote, pink feldspar, and quartz.
Common source: Republic of South Africa
Astrological association: Scorpio
Chakra: Heart
Healing: Grief (especially for the loss of an idea or dream), fertility

Crystal Connections

Keywords: Self-imposed blocks, letting go, being free
Crystal talk: Unakite wants you to be in the present, to experience this moment. It talks of letting go of the past and anything that is holding you back. Unakite often ties to people who may be living or have passed on to the next world. It is all about acceptance and not judgment. Accept your past and everything that has happened and let it all go—release it to the Universe. Then you are free to experience every moment for its own worth.

Chrysocolla

Description: Forms layers, masses, botryoidal structures, and druses. Blue/green in color, often with inclusions of other minerals such as cuprite, quartz, malachite, shattuckite, and so on.
Common sources: Peru, USA
Astrological associations: Taurus, Gemini, Virgo
Chakra: Heart
Healing: Female reproductive system, menstrual cycle, PMS, development of foetus, arthritis, digestion

Crystal Connections

Keywords: Stress, phobias, tension, guilt, troubled mind
Crystal talk: Chrysocolla is almost always formed as a mixed mineral and as such is looking at everything it sees from many different angles. At first, this can seem confusing, as you may appear to be receiving contradictory pieces of advice. However, when you take a step back and listen to what this crystal says, it becomes clear that you are seeing situations from different sides, giving you the information you need to make a decision.

Amazonite

Description: A yellow- to blue-green variety of microcline (a variety of feldspar), forming crystals and masses.
Common sources: Brazil, Russia, USA
Astrological association: Virgo
Chakra: Heart
Healing: Nerves, nervous system

Crystal Connections

Keywords: A "feel-better" stone, happiness, creativity, stress, nervousness
Crystal talk: Amazonite's message is always about stilling your nerves. If you feel stressed and automatically become

nervous, then this is the stone for you! It suggests you calm down, relax, and don't worry—this too shall pass. It tells you not to let stress get the better of you because you can cope with everything, but sometimes you just need a little help and that's what this crystal is here to do. The first time I worked with amazonite with a client, they had arrived for the session very shaken from a near accident on the way. They were physically shaking. I didn't know why at the time, but had an irresistible urge to place amazonite in their hands. Within minutes they had stopped shaking and visibly started to relax.

Green calcite

Description: Bright emerald to pale green masses
Common source: Mexico
Astrological association: Cancer
Chakra: Heart
Healing: Prevention and treatment of infection

Crystal Connections

Keywords: Emotion, anxiety, panic attacks
Crystal talk: Green calcite wins the prize for the most instantly calming crystal. Whatever is going on, it will be with you. I regularly place green calcite in a new client's hands during treatments when they are unsure what to expect. And if anyone is panicking, it will quickly soothe them. Green calcite feels so smooth in the hand and this is the feeling it imparts to anyone holding it. Having said that, it will occasionally touch something deep inside, so don't be surprised if you do not feel great when you have this crystal around. Green calcite reminds us that it is part of the healing process to let things go.

Emerald

Description: A green gem variety of beryl that forms hexagonal prismatic crystals with flat or, occasionally, small pyramidal terminations.
Common sources: Colombia (gem quality), Brazil (commercial grade)
Astrological associations: Aries, Taurus, Gemini
Chakra: Heart
Healing: Vitality, liver, memory, eyesight, immune system

Crystal Connections

Keywords: Fertility, growth, patience, honesty
Crystal talk: Emerald speaks of the heart, of love of every kind, lovers, friends, family, pets, nature, and important things. It will open your heart to the possibilities in all sorts of relationships in your life. Emerald also wants you to love everything you do, whether it is at home, on vacation, at work or at play. Life should be fun and emerald says to open your heart and embrace all there is in your world.

Bowenite

Description: Fine, granular, green masses of antigorite
Alternate name: New jade
Common sources: China, USA
Astrological association: Aquarius
Chakra: Heart
Healing: Heart, cholesterol

Crystal Connections

Keywords: Stone of the warrior, affording protection and releasing the past and self-imposed blocks

Crystal talk: Bowenite likes challenges! We grow and strengthen from the trials in our lives. But we often stop ourselves from taking the first step in an adventure and choose the known and well-worn path instead. Bowenite reminds you when you are doing this and blocking your own path to new things. It can help remove the barricades you place around you to protect you from past hurts. It says the past has gone; it is time to be brave and move on.

Chrysoprase

Description: A green variety of chalcedony. Can also be yellow, in which case it is known as lemon chrysoprase or lemon chalcedony.
Common sources: Australia, Brazil, Germany, Poland, Russia, Tanzania, USA (Arizona and California)
Astrological association: Libra
Chakra: Heart
Healing: Mental health and healing, makes you feel better.

Crystal Connections

Keywords: Helps you to see through the fog in your mind, acceptance

Crystal talk: I could not understand how it was that my client was progressing so slowly. Several treatments in and I heard a voice calling me. I left my client in the therapy room and went into my adjacent store to see who was calling. I was drawn to this beautiful, translucent, green tumble polished stone that was literally glowing with light. I placed this stone on my client's brow chakra and she instantly and visibly relaxed. After the treatment she said it was as if a gentle breeze had blown through her mind, the fog cleared in her brain, and she could hear what the chrysoprase was saying. By the following week's treatment, she had shifted her life by accepting and moving on.

Peridot

Description: Small, green prismatic crystals and masses. Also red, brown, and yellow.
Common sources: Afghanistan, Brazil, Canary Islands, Pakistan, Russia, Sri Lanka, USA
Astrological associations: Leo, Virgo, Scorpio, Sagittarius
Chakra: Heart
Healing: Digestion, detoxing, acidity, addictions

Crystal Connections

Keywords: Lethargy, anger, depression

Crystal talk: Peridot speaks of feeling better and being happy. Let go of the negatives holding you back and share the joy. It reminds you that like attracts like, so if you're feeling down, you draw others with the same depressed predisposition as you. Similarly, if you have a sparkly and happy outlook, then you will meet people who feel like that too. Peridot reminds us to be ourselves and not let outside influences become overbearing, and to avoid repeating unhelpful behavior patterns and cycles.

Moldavite

Description: Green tektite was created when a meteorite exploded above the Earth's surface, melting both itself and the surface of the Earth. This is the resulting reformed natural glass material: part Earth, part alien. Moldavite is the only green tektite.
Only source: Czech Republic
Astrological associations: All
Chakra: Brow and heart
Healing: Mental and physical balance

Crystal Connections

Keywords: Openness, change, possibilities
Crystal talk: Moldavite tells you to open your mind and take off the shackles of limitation. It reminds you that if you can imagine it, you can create it, and it helps you to look at anything from different angles of possibility. Moldavite beckons you to try new things and to feel these experiences with your whole being. Be in the moment and trust clairsentient sensations (those acquired through psychic feeling). This crystal says, "If I can get here from billions of light years away, what you are doing is a walk in the park." He then takes your hand and guides you along your Yellow Brick Road.

Green tourmaline

Description: A green variety of tourmaline that forms vertically striated prismatic crystals.
Alternate name: Verdelite
Common sources: Brazil, Pakistan, Afghanistan, Mozambique, Namibia, Nigeria
Astrological association: Capricorn
Chakra: Heart, brow
Healing: Protection, worry, immune system

Crystal Connections

Keywords: Peace of mind
Crystal talk: Green tourmaline speaks of the green shoots of new beginnings, leading to success and bringing abundance on many levels. It tells you that you are protected and safe, and there is no need to worry. Do everything you can about any situation and then close the door as you leave your metaphorical office (or your real office!). This tourmaline will bring confidence if you follow its advice. Shed any negativity that might be holding you back and shoot for the stars!

PINK

Rose quartz

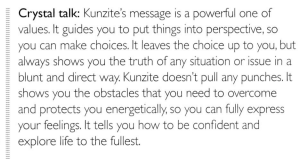

Description: Pink crystalline masses and, rarely, small, hexagonal crystals
Common sources: Brazil, India, Madagascar, Republic of South Africa
Astrological associations: Taurus, Libra
Chakra: Heart
Healing: Fertility, heart, general aches and pains, skin

Crystal Connections

Keywords: Love, creativity, art, beauty
Crystal talk: Rose quartz expresses love and connection. All kinds of love and all types of interactions. It whispers words such as forgiveness and tolerance that allow relationships to repair. And it advises letting go of anger and phobias, and releasing fear, guilt, jealousy, and resentment to bring partnerships to their fullest and closest potential. If you are creative, then rose quartz will guide you in art and music, or writing poetry, fact, or fiction. It will help you to trust your heart and act accordingly. It tells you to open your heart and embrace the world in love, laughter, and happiness.

Kunzite

Description: A pink variety of spodumene that forms flattened prismatic crystals with vertical striations. Other colors include blue, green, clear, lilac, or yellow. Crystals may also be bicolor and tricolor.
Common sources: Afghanistan, Brazil
Astrological associations: Scorpio, Taurus, Libra, Aries, Leo
Chakra: Heart
Healing: Addictions (both physical and behavioral), cycles and patterns

Crystal Connections

Keywords: Expression of love, a "feel-better" crystal

Crystal talk: Kunzite's message is a powerful one of values. It guides you to put things into perspective, so you can make choices. It leaves the choice up to you, but always shows you the truth of any situation or issue in a blunt and direct way. Kunzite doesn't pull any punches. It shows you the obstacles that you need to overcome and protects you energetically, so you can fully express your feelings. It tells you how to be confident and explore life to the fullest.

Pink opal

Description: Pink masses that may exhibit iridescence.
Common source: Peru
Astrological association: Cancer
Chakra: Heart
Healing: Reproductive system, diabetes, skin

Crystal Connections

Keywords: Rebirth, awakening, renewal
Crystal talk: The first thing pink opal says is to clear your mind. Take a few deep breaths and slow down. It tells you that once you give yourself a minute to think, you will see that you need to start to heal yourself before you can find your true vocation and help others on their path. Just as I did, so many healers started healing others because of their own experiences. Open your eyes and experience your rebirth as a spiritual being having an earthly existence. Pink opal tells you that when you realize this, you will find love, happiness, and peace.

Pink banded agate

Description: A variety of agate with pink, white, and gray banding and patterns.
Common source: Botswana
Astrological associations: Taurus, Scorpio
Chakra: Heart, sacral
Healing: Nervousness, stress, detoxing

Crystal Connections

Keywords: Inner goddess, femininity, creativity, nurture
Crystal talk: Pink banded agate shows you your inner

goddess and tells you exactly how to connect with her. She ties in with the feminine qualities we all have, such as nurturing, creativity and spontaneity, whichever gender we are, and helps you to express these. Whenever I have difficulty seeing through a complex situation, I sit quietly with my pink banded agate, and she reminds me to pay attention to the details. She'll prompt me to look at the whole picture to find the best solution.

Rhodochrosite

Description: Found as masses, druses, botryoidal structures, and, rarely, rhombohedral crystals. Colors range from deep to pale pink, deep red, yellow, orange, and brown.
Common sources: Argentina, Peru, Republic of South Africa, Russia, China, Gabonese Republic, Mexico, Japan, USA (Montana)
Astrological associations: Leo, Scorpio
Chakra: Heart
Healing: Heart, circulation, ME (myalgic encephalomyelitis), healthy development of babies

Crystal Connections

Keywords: Passion, sex, making music
Crystal talk: Rhodochrosite talks of passion for life and everything you do. Its message is to go with the flow in everything you do, as this makes your life much easier and more fun and leads to greater success. It reminds you to avoid causing stresses you don't already have to materialize in your life. I call this specific type of stress "21st-century stress." It is caused when you are running around trying to achieve too much in too little time, doing everything to keep everyone else happy—except yourself. Rhodochrosite screams at you "STOP!" Then calmly and quietly tells you to start again, doing everything from this moment on with passion from your heart and soul.

Rhodonite

Description: Pink or red masses and tabular crystals. Other colors include green, yellow, and black, often with black lines which are veined manganese inclusions.
Common sources: Australia, Brazil, Canada, India, Madagascar, Peru, Republic of South Africa, Sweden, UK (Cornwall), USA (North Carolina, Colorado)
Astrological association: Taurus
Chakra: Heart
Healing: Heart, bones, mental balance, ME (myalgic encephalomyelitis)

Crystal Connections

Keywords: Making music, unconditional love
Crystal talk: Rhodonite is a stone of music and speaks of rhythms in everything you do (I have a massive piece in my recording studio!). It relays ancient tales of a spiritual love that is unconditional and shared without limits. Rhodonite tells you to ground your feelings of love in the physical world. It says that it is okay to be sensitive and feel what others are feeling, but without stressing yourself. It suggests that you simply replace the self-stress with self-esteem and become a confident, balanced, and healthy person.

Cobaltoan calcite

Description: Forms druses, spherical masses, and, rarely, crystals.
Common sources: Democratic Republic of Congo, Morocco
Astrological association: Cancer
Chakra: Heart, throat, brow, crown
Healing: Emotional expression

Crystal Connections

Keywords: Seeing the beauty in everything
Crystal talk: Cobaltoan calcite reminds you that in every person and any situation there is always beauty, which you can choose to see or not. It inspires you to acknowledge and learn the lessons

you are presented with along your path in life, so you can discover your inner truth and purpose. To do this, it will tell you to bring past hurts to the fore, so you can release the emotional pain associated with them and free yourself. Then it will be easier to see the beauty in everything.

Morganite

Description: A pink variety of beryl that forms hexagonal prismatic crystals with flat or, occasionally, small pyramidal terminations.
Common sources: Brazil, Pakistan, Afghanistan, Mozambique, Namibia
Astrological association: Libra
Chakra: Heart
Healing: Respiratory issues

Crystal Connections

Keywords: Love, wisdom, clarity
Crystal talk: A wise crystal once said, "Bring wisdom and clear thought." This helps you to see a different perspective. Morganite exudes love and tells you the kind and gentle words you need to fill the spaces left in your heart from a broken relationship or a death. It tells you there is more to be found and that you are valued and worthy of loving and of beautiful people and things in your life.

Strawberry quartz

Description: A pink variety of massive quartz, the color of crushed strawberries
Common source: Republic of South Africa
Astrological association: Libra
Chakra: Heart, crown
Healing: Channels away excess energy you are not using—can relieve mysterious symptoms that seem to have no cause, such as headaches and palpitations.

Crystal Connections

Keywords: Reality, truth
Crystal talk: Strawberry quartz reminds me of summer. And, just like summer, things don't tend to last forever. It tells you to be realistic and let things go, reminds you that this is a natural flow of events, and just as summer becomes fall, so fall turns into winter, so winter turns into spring, and spring becomes summer. Strawberry quartz says that life is a cycle and, as it tells you this, you can begin to relax, find your place of calm, and bring peace to your mind.

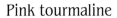

Pink tourmaline

Description: Hexagonal striated, pink to red crystals, often growing in other minerals such as quartz or lepidolite.
Alternate name: Rubellite
Common sources: Australia, Brazil, Madagascar, Namibia, Pakistan, Republic of South Africa
Astrological associations: Taurus, Libra, Scorpio, Sagittarius
Chakra: Heart
Healing: Heart, lungs, digestion, fertility

Crystal Connections

Keywords: Replenishes love
Crystal talk: One of my clients was going through a rough patch in her personal relationship. I gave her a piece of pink tourmaline to help her. She put it under her pillow and told me that the crystal spoke to her in a dream. In her dream, the pink tourmaline advised her how to solve the problem, step by step, and to leave the relationship, with each step making the transition acceptable for both her and her partner. Both of them are now content with their separate lives. Pink tourmaline has words of wisdom for any problem that needs resolving.

RAINBOW AND MULTICOLORED CRYSTALS

Labradorite

Description: Masses and, rarely, tabular crystals of plagioclase feldspar with albite. Colors include colorless, gray-green, pale green, blue, gray-white, or golden, all with brilliant flashes of blue, red, gold, green, and purple due to light interference within the structure of the mineral's composition known as labradorescence.
Common sources: Madagascar, Canada, Norway, Finland, China, Australia, Slovakia, USA
Astrological associations: Leo, Scorpio, Sagittarius
Chakra: Crown
Healing: Aura

Crystal Connections

Keywords: Inspiration, intuition, intellect, ideas
Crystal talk: Whenever I carry labradorite, things just seem to happen without effort. When labradorite is around there is always magic in the air. It says to just be, keep doing what you are doing, and trust the Universe; then  magic can happen around you. It will inspire you to see magical opportunities, which are there, although sometimes you simply don't see them. Open your eyes and your heart, and your mind will follow. Labradorite helps you to see the mystical possibilities in its shimmering colors.

Fire agate

Description: Brownish pebbles with colorful flashes of "fire" due to thin layers of limonite
Common source: Mexico
Astrological association: Aries
Chakra: Brow
Healing: Eyes

Crystal Connections

Keywords: Inspiration, action
Crystal talk: Fire agate calls on otherworldly friends, such as spirit guides and guardian angels, to help you when you need it. It helps you find your direction and protects you as you travel along your path, helping you to see your truth on all levels. Not only does it inspire ideas, but it also says to get up and go, giving you a gentle kick up the backside when you are procrastinating! Fire agate tells you to open your eyes and see things as they truly are.

Chalcopyrite

Description: Occurs as octahedral crystals, masses, and tetrahedral crystals with sphenoid faces. Usually in bright iridescent colors, including gold, blue, green, and purple—often in the same specimen—which are produced by natural surface oxidation. Scratching may remove the bright colors to reveal gray rock, which will oxidize naturally again to produce colors in the right environment over time.

Common sources: Brazil, Mexico
Astrological association: Capricorn
Chakra: Crown
Healing: Improves the flow of chi, so helps with many issues.

Crystal Connections

Keywords: Flow, healing, release
Crystal talk: When you have chalcopyrite with you, things tend to flow better, so be prepared to grasp opportunities and run with them. Change does not flow evenly, surging and receding as it is happening. One day, everything is just ticking along, then, the next, your whole world can seem upside down. The trick is to go with the flow; this will speed up any changes and reduce any discomfort they may bring, allowing you to make the most of the quieter days in your life. Chalcopyrite is calling on you to embrace the changes.

Opal

Description: Masses in a multitude of colors, including white, pink, black, blue, beige, yellow, brown, orange, red, green, and purple. There is sometimes iridescence showing fire in multiple colors, which is produced by the diffraction of light within the crystalline structure. Common opal (also white) does not have a diffraction grating in its structure and, as a result, shows no color.
Common sources: Australia, Peru, USA, Ethiopia, Mexico, Indonesia, Czech Republic
Astrological associations: Cancer, Libra, Scorpio, Pisces
Chakra: Heart, throat, crown
Healing: Eyes, vision, childbirth, detoxing

Crystal Connections

Keywords: Creativity, inspiration, imagination, memory
Crystal talk: Opal helps us to see things as they are—to see through the veil of confusion that is often present in troubling situations. It tells you to be you—that unique and amazing person—and not to follow the crowd. Free your inhibitions and in the same way that some people mistakenly believe opals to be unlucky, so you do not need to be concerned about what others might mistakenly think about you. It speaks of the past and your connection to your ancestors, the land, nature, and the future. Opal is optimistic.

Rainbow fluorite

Description: A multicolored variety of fluorite that forms cubic or octahedral crystals and masses.
Common sources: China, Mexico
Astrological association: Pisces
Chakra: Heart, throat, brow, crown
Healing: Teeth, gums, and a general tonic

Crystal Connections

Keywords: Focus, clarity, mind
Crystal talk: Rainbow fluorite shows us the many layers of any argument. When you are confused, and your mind is struggling for clarity, it will help you to focus and clear the fog of confusion. It reminds you to keep the sun behind you. That way, you will always have an advantage. Of course, it is talking metaphorically and telling you always to find the best place to make your stand, so you have a natural advantage. It also speaks of clarity and clear communication when you need to get your point across.

Watermelon tourmaline

Description: A green or blue, longitudinally striated tourmaline with a pink or red center running through all or part of the crystal.
Common sources: Brazil, Pakistan, Afghanistan, Nigeria, Madagascar, USA (Maine)
Astrological associations: Gemini, Virgo
Chakra: Heart
Healing: A powerful emotional healer

Crystal Connections

Keywords: Love, fun, humor, feeling better
Crystal talk: Watermelon tourmaline reminds you to do everything from your heart. Live your life full of passion, joy, laughter, and fun. Open your heart to all and share the wonderfully deep love you have inside. It will guide you through emotional difficulties and show you that in spite of anything that may have happened in the past, the future can be filled with love and happiness.

Titanium quartz

Description: A variety of quartz crystal bonded with titanium and niobium.
Common sources: USA, Brazil, China
Astrological associations: All
Chakra: All
Healing: Chronic conditions

Crystal Connections

Keywords: Change, seeing alternatives
Crystal talk: Titanium quartz helps you to focus on your career and encourages you to make the changes you need to be successful and happy. It tells you to avoid rigidity in your thoughts and emotions and to be open to innovative ideas. It will always show you other people's points of view and then let you decide on your own route along your career path. However, this crystal will not dictate to you; it will only put possible options in front of you. It says that it is always up to you to make the changes you need and want in your life.

Angel aura quartz

Description: A variety of quartz crystal bonded with platinum and silver.
Common sources: USA, Brazil, China
Astrological asssociations: All
Chakra: All
Healing: Nurture, caring, holding

Crystal Connections

Keywords: Harmony, love, peace, angels
Crystal talk: As the name suggests, angel aura quartz crystals help you connect to your angels and the angelic realms in general. There, you can find answers to almost any question. It is guiding you to where you will find the answers you need. When you carry or wear angel aura quartz, you start to see signposts around you in everyday things, guiding you safely through the world. These signs are always there, but this crystal shows you where to look for them. Angel aura quartz is particularly helpful to healers and those of you in the caring professions, increasing your natural empathy while also protecting your energy, so you do not get drained in the process of helping people.

BLUE

Blue lace agate

Description: A pale blue and white banded variety of agate.
Common source: Namibia
Astrological association: Pisces
Chakra: Throat
Healing: Throat, speech, eyesight, trapped nerves

Crystal Connections

Keywords: Communication, peacefulness
Crystal talk: Blue lace agate brings peace and harmony. This is its message in any scenario. It tells us to take the path of least resistance and least argument, but never to be afraid to speak your truth. Blue lace agate reminds you that speaking honestly about your feelings is always the best course to take. It will dissolve any problems you have around communicating, especially spiritual ideas.

Blue chalcedony

Description: A light blue variety of chalcedony forming masses.
Common sources: Namibia, Turkey, USA (Montana)
Astrological associations: Cancer, Sagittarius
Chakra: Throat
Healing: Childhood issues

Crystal Connections

Keywords: Childhood, past lives
Crystal talk: Blue chalcedony helps you recall your past, so you can learn from its lessons. It will tell you how to overcome any issues rooted in your past, especially in your childhood or past lives. Blue chalcedony tells you what your aura holds in its files about you; that is, everything there is to know. It will then let you know the best things to do in order to heal. It will also give you the words you need to express your true feelings.

Blue apatite

Description: Blue to blue-green, opaque to translucent prismatic crystals
Common sources: Brazil, Madagascar, Myanmar, Mexico, Canada
Astrological association: Gemini
Chakra: Throat
Healing: Weight control, taste, smell, hearing, sight

Crystal Connections

Keywords: Individuality, communication of ideas
Crystal talk: Blue apatite tells you to take your idea and run with it. This crystal is all about communicating your ideas and it will protect your aura as you step out to do this. Beware falling into the trap of copying other people and stick to your own unique ideas, even if they sometimes feel a bit off the wall. Blue apatite reminds you to bask in your individuality and find your harmonious and peaceful life path, and then to start taking steps along that path toward your bright and happy future. It will guide you through troubling times after loss or disaster, reminding you that you have the inner strength and deep courage to overcome.

THE POWER TO COMMUNICATE

Blue crystals, as a generalization, aid communication. Some, such as blue lace agate and aquamarine, will calm your words, helping you to find kinder ways of expressing the deepest feelings sitting in your heart. Whereas others, like kyanite and lapis lazuli, can help you cut through other people's nonsense, getting quickly and directly to the point. Some help you express issues from your childhood like blue chalcedony and blue calcite; others, such as celestite and sapphire, help you communicate with guides and angels. Still others such as tanzanite and blue tourmaline will help you express the ideas drifting in your mind.

Kyanite

Description: Blade-type crystals, fibers, and masses. Colors include blue, black, green, orange, gray, white, yellow, and pink.
Common sources: Worldwide—especially Brazil, Myanmar, Mexico, Republic of South Africa, Namibia, Kenya
Astrological associations: Aries, Taurus, Libra
Chakra: Throat
Healing: Communication, voice, aligns chakras

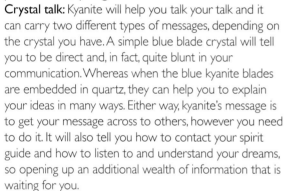

Crystal Connections

Keywords: Expression, perseverance, spirit guides
Crystal talk: Kyanite will help you talk your talk and it can carry two different types of messages, depending on the crystal you have. A simple blue blade crystal will tell you to be direct and, in fact, quite blunt in your communication. Whereas when the blue kyanite blades are embedded in quartz, they can help you to explain your ideas in many ways. Either way, kyanite's message is to get your message across to others, however you need to do it. It will also tell you how to contact your spirit guide and how to listen to and understand your dreams, so opening up an additional wealth of information that is waiting for you.

Aquamarine

Description: A blue/green variety of beryl that forms hexagonal prismatic crystals with flat or, occasionally, small pyramidal terminations.
Common sources: Afghanistan, Brazil, Namibia, Pakistan, USA, Nigeria, Madagascar, Republic of Zambia, Mozambique
Astrological associations: Aries, Gemini, Pisces
Chakra: Throat
Healing: Bodily fluids (such as blood and lymph), swelling, fluid retention

Crystal Connections

Keywords: Traveling, intellect, study, communication, courage
Crystal talk: Aquamarine can feel unbelievably soft and gentle when it shares comforting words, but do not be fooled, because although just like its color, it can be gentle and calming, it can also whisper words of courage and strength when you need them to make things happen for you. It is a traveler and carries powerful tales of magical journeys and adventure to strengthen and inspire you as well as provide you with loving support—aquamarine always has a helpful story for you when you are packing for a journey. It also has a very direct way of speaking the truth about yourself.

Angelite

Description: Blue/white nodules and masses
Common source: Peru
Astrological association: Aquarius
Chakra: Throat
Healing: Senses (hearing, taste, touch, sight, smell)

Crystal Connections

Keywords: Awareness, communication, security, angels
Crystal talk: Some people say angels speak through angelite. Personally, I have found that it always has the right thing to say at the right time. So much so that you may find it easier to express your feelings. If you suffer loss, it will talk you through the five stages of grief (denial, anger, bargaining, depression, acceptance) and help you to communicate with your angels and other spirit guardians. Angelite likes talking to animals too. If you are having trouble understanding a pet, take angelite with you and it will translate dog or cat, or whatever the animal's language, into one you can understand.

Blue calcite

Description: Blue masses
Common sources: Mexico, Argentina
Astrological association: Cancer
Chakra: Throat
Healing: Calming (especially helpful for children)

Crystal Connections

Keywords: Inner child, calm communication
Crystal talk: Blue calcite has calming tales for adults and children. It talks to your inner child, reassuring and calming your spirit. Blue calcite has a happy and optimistic tone that gives you a feeling of safety. It always seems to have the right words at the right time for anyone.

Celestite

Description: Tabular orthorhombic crystals, nodules, and masses in shades of blue. Crystals can also be found in yellow, white, orange, red, and red-brown.
Common source: Madagascar
Astrological association: Gemini
Chakra: Brow
Healing: Speech, mental health

Crystal Connections

Keywords: Creative expression, clarity, dreams, angels
Crystal talk: Celestite is good for hearing and so it will promote itself and help you hear its messages. These often come to you in dreams. I find that when I place my celestite on my nightstand (bedside table), my dreams are clearer and I can recall every detail without missing anything out. Celestite always speaks of respect in everything it does—respect for the planet, for nature, for partners and peers, and people in general. You can also ask your angels for guidance and celestite will translate their angelic messages.

Lapis lazuli

Description: Rock, cubic, and dodecahedral crystals and masses, almost always with inclusions of lazurite, calcite, and pyrite.
Common sources: Afghanistan, Chile
Astrological association: Sagittarius
Chakra: Brow
Healing: Immune system, broken and fractured bones, muscles

Crystal Connections

Keywords: Structure, awareness
Crystal talk: Lapis lazuli tells you to open your mind, so you can open your heart. It does everything it can to end narrow-mindedness and bigotry of any kind. It speaks of openness, friendship, and love, and it does this by making you more aware, so you can see the truth for yourself in any situation. Then you can open your heart to all. That is a beautiful place to be. And this is lapis lazuli's message.

Aqua aura

Description: A quartz crystal bonded with gold, creating vivid blue, mostly transparent, crystals.
Common sources: USA, Brazil, China
Astrological association: Leo
Chakra: Brow, throat
Healing: Trauma, aura

Crystal Connections

Keywords: Communication, dispels negativity
Crystal talk: This is a chatty crystal that wants to say something to cheer you up when you're feeling low, so you will feel better. Many years ago, I was in my crystal store when there was a traffic accident outside. I didn't see it, but I heard it. A few minutes later a lady came in traumatized and with blood over her clothes. I quickly ascertained that the blood was not hers and that she had helped someone else who had been knocked down. As soon as I realized this, I heard a crystal calling to me and I looked round to see aqua aura shining away in its brilliant blueness. Up until then, I had always seen it as a crystal to help you feel happier when you are sad for any reason, to support and heal your aura, and to help communication on many levels, which is more or less what I expressed in my first book *The Crystal Healer*. However, I listened to this crystal and gave it to the lady to hold. Within minutes, I could see the trauma draining from her and she started to get herself back together. It was incredible to observe.

Sapphire

Description: Commonly a blue gem variety of corundum, but can be any color except red (which is ruby). Usually forms hexagonal, barrel-shaped, flat-terminated crystals.
Common sources: India, Afghanistan, Sri Lanka, Madagascar, Thailand, Myanmar, Laos, Vietnam, Australia, China, Colombia, Ethiopia, Tanzania, Rwanda, Nigeria, Kenya
Astrological associations: Virgo, Libra, Sagittarius
Chakra: Brow
Healing: Glands

Crystal Connections

Keywords: Ambition, dreams, goals
Crystal talk: Sapphire supports your dreams and gives you hints for the best or easiest ways of achieving them. People might think you are psychic, as you start to pre-empt potential problems on your path and circumnavigate them with ease. Sapphire can boost your communication with your spirit guides, translating their energies into vibrations that you can hear. "Record keeper" sapphires can also connect you to a wealth of wisdom held in the Akashic records (an unwritten compendium of each past, present, and future thought, word, and deed of every living being).

Tanzanite

Description: A variety of zoisite that forms striated prismatic crystals and masses. Colors include blue, yellow, gray/blue, and purple. Some crystals may be bicolor and/or birefringent.
Common source: Tanzania
Astrological associations: Gemini, Libra, Sagittarius
Chakra: Throat, brow, crown
Healing: Skin, eyes, emotional exhaustion

Crystal Connections

Keywords: Communication, meditation, magic
Crystal talk: Tanzanite says that anything is possible! Somehow, on those odd occasions when I am stuck on a project, I pick up my tanzanite crystal and listen to what he has to say. He always tells me the next step that will unblock the road to success. I have a tanzanite Buddha who also helps me to meditate, translating my thoughts into images. I work with him to develop guided meditations and visualizations.

Turquoise

Description: Blue, green, or blue/green masses, crusts, and, rarely, small prismatic crystals
Common sources: USA, Mexico, Chile, China, Myanmar, Iran
Astrological associations: Scorpio, Sagittarius, Pisces
Chakra: Throat
Healing: Allergies, mutipurpose healer

Crystal Connections

Keywords: Possibilities, opportunities, balance, spirituality
Crystal talk: In some American First Nation cultures there is a belief that we walk along two roads simultaneously: the Red Road and the Blue Road. The Red Road is the Earth plane. That's your usual, everyday life that you see around you. In contrast, the Blue Road is the path your spirit travels on. It is the Blue Road that opens possibilities in the Red Road, and listening to your own spirit (soul) will always show you the right signs to follow. Turquoise translates these signs, so you can understand them as you travel along your Red Road.

Blue tourmaline

Description: A blue variety of tourmaline that forms vertically striated prismatic crystals.
Alternate name: Indicolite
Common sources: Brazil, Nigeria, Afghanistan
Astrological associations: Taurus, Libra
Chakra: Throat, brow
Healing: Breathing, breath

Crystal Connections

Keywords: Environment, communication, intuition
Crystal talk: Blue tourmaline helps you talk your talk and walk your walk. Many people setting out on a spiritual or holistic path can encounter resistance from family and friends who may not understand what they are doing. I was lucky enough to come across indicolite early on my crystal journey and its guiding voice helped me navigate what could otherwise have been a sea of anguish. It said that I should continue what I was doing and keep talking to everyone about it! This crystal will also tell you what to say to whom and how to say it to get your message across.

VIOLET

Amethyst

Description: A purple variety of quartz found as crystals or masses. Its classic purple color is due to manganese and iron inclusions.
Common sources: Brazil, Uruguay, Republic of South Africa, Madagascar, India, USA, Republic of Zambia
Astrological associations: Virgo, Capricorn, Aquarius, Pisces
Chakra: Crown
Healing: Physical, emotional, and mental balance, headaches, insomnia, infections

Crystal Connections

Keywords: Mindset, direction, letting go, living in the moment, spiritual connection
Crystal talk: Amethyst focuses your mindset, helping you to find your purpose and direction. It is asking, "What's your next move?" Dispel fears, worries, and past events that might be holding you back. Amethyst

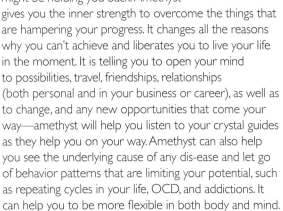

gives you the inner strength to overcome the things that are hampering your progress. It changes all the reasons why you can't achieve and liberates you to live your life in the moment. It is telling you to open your mind to possibilities, travel, friendships, relationships (both personal and in your business or career), as well as to change, and any new opportunities that come your way—amethyst will help you listen to your crystal guides as they help you on your way. Amethyst can also help you see the underlying cause of any dis-ease and let go of behavior patterns that are limiting your potential, such as repeating cycles in your life, OCD, and addictions. It can help you to be more flexible in both body and mind.

Lepidolite

Description: Found as masses and layered plates ("books") and short prismatic and tabular crystals. Usually lavender (pink to purple), but may also be colorless, yellow, gray, or white.

Common source: Brazil
Astrological association: Libra
Chakra: Heart, brow
Healing: Mental health, addictions, study, change

Crystal Connections

Keywords: Learning, digesting ideas, understanding, release
Crystal talk: Lepidolite often forms layered plates, which are known as "books." They can act just like a book, allowing you to gain information continuously and on many levels. These books help you to digest ideas and turn them into

practical growth. You can also let go of self-limiting ideas and create powerful wishes by writing them in a Lepidolite Wishing Book (see box below). The underlying message is that it's okay to trust the Universe.

LEPIDOLITE WISHING BOOK

Hold a crystal wand in your dominant hand as you would write with a pen. Hold your lepidolite book crystal in your other hand. You can work with any variety of crystal wand for this, but I prefer to use a selenite or quartz crystal.

Hold your crystal wand with the point approximately 1 cm (½ in.) above the surface of the lepidolite book. Above the left page of the book, "write" a list of the things you stop yourself doing and, if you can, why you do this. Above the right page, write down all you wish for.

When you have finished, put the wand down, hold the book between your hands, and ask the lepidolite crystal to transform the negatives on the left page into the positive wishes on the right. Picture all your wishes coming true.

Super Seven

Description: A variety of included quartz comprising seven different minerals: amethyst, cacoxenite, goethite, lepidocrocite, quartz, rutile, and smoky quartz. Usually purple is the main color, but, because of the inclusions, areas of the crystal may look brown, red, white, black, or colorless. Small pieces will exhibit all the qualities, even if all seven minerals are not present in the specimen: the original mass giving super seven its amazing voice.
Alternate names: Super 7, sacred seven, the Melody stone (after my dear friend, Melody, the American crystal healer and author)
Only source: Espírito Santo, Brazil
Astrological associations: All
Chakra: All
Healing: Nervous system, aura

Crystal Connections

Keywords: Connection, spirit, truth, awareness
Crystal talk: Super seven is the crystal to help you follow your dreams, its words guiding you toward the fulfillment of your hopes, goals, and positive desires. It boosts psychic abilities, which we all have, and its message changes how we view our world—we can listen to the answers it gives to those things we thought were problems. For the brave, it can also speed the law of Karma, freeing us from past issues and events, from this life or past lives, which might be holding us back and stopping us reaching our fullest potential.

Purple fluorite

Description: A purple variety of fluorite. The Mexican crystals often form "crystal castles."
Common sources: China, Mexico
Astrological associations: Capricorn, Pisces
Chakra: Crown
Healing: Mouth, teeth and gums, bones and bone marrow

Crystal Connections

Keywords: Communication, focusing the mind, new lessons
Crystal talk: When you empty your mind and focus on purple fluorite, you can see the structure that holds your thoughts together, even when they feel disparate and you feel lost. It can also help you understand the spiritual reasons for dis-ease and the path you are destined to follow in this lifetime. Once you have learned this, purple fluorite is excellent at helping you communicate these lessons to others, whether casually in conversation, or more formally teaching classes and workshops or giving public talks and lectures. Purple fluorite is telling you to get up off your backside and do what you know you need to do!

Sugilite

Description: Violet masses and, rarely, tiny crystals
Common sources: Republic of South Africa
Astrological association: Virgo
Chakra: Crown
Healing: Mental health, mind–body link in dis-ease

Crystal Connections

Keywords: Confidence, creativity, courage
Crystal talk: Sugilite wants you to find your role in life, your life path. It tells you the things you need to hear in order to strengthen your

confidence and give you the courage required to succeed in troubling times. With sugilite you will find the soft words you need to fully express yourself without upsetting others and thus avert hostility, anger, jealousy, and prejudice.

Spirit quartz

Description: A variety of amethyst (purple) or quartz (white or clear) encrusted with numerous small crystals of the same mineral, each with a termination. May also appear orange/brown due to iron inclusions or surface staining.
Only source: Republic of South Africa
Astrological associations: Virgo, Capricorn, Aquarius, Pisces
Chakra: Crown
Healing: Family relationships

Crystal Connections

Keywords: Patience, teams, fertility
Crystal talk: Spirit quartz talks of families, friends, and teamwork. It tells you how to pull everyone together to achieve your desired goal. Spirit quartz brings with it the people skills and understanding you require, as well as the words you will need to hold everybody together and get them paddling the canoe in unison along your river, sitting in the flow of energy and avoiding any rocks and rapids along the way.

Banded amethyst

Description: Crystals and masses with purple and white banding in a chevron pattern.
Alternate name: Chevron amethyst
Common sources: Brazil, India, Russia, Zambia
Astrological associations: All
Chakra: Brow, crown
Healing: Chronic pain

Crystal Connections

Keywords: Exploration of your emotions, understanding, breakthrough, normality
Crystal talk: Due to a digestive condition and much surgery in consequence, I have continuous chronic pain. When I first started working with banded amethyst, it took the edge off the pain, which made so many things more bearable, but then it also started to help me explore my relationship with the pain. It showed me how to change my mindset from one of allowing the pain to control everything I did—or, more to the point, didn't do—to breaking free from its control and getting on with my life. It can also guide you on your spiritual path, and your connection to nature.

CLEAR AND WHITE

Rainbow moonstone

Description: A white variety of feldspar that exhibits a schiller effect—adularescence that can give the stone a blue sheen and make it appear to glow gently inside.
Common source: India
Astrological association: Cancer
Chakra: Sacral, crown
Healing: Fertility, lunar cycles, and physical and emotional effects

Crystal Connections

Keywords: Inner goddess, creativity, cleansing
Crystal talk: Rainbow moonstone will remind you to reconnect with Mother Earth. It tells you that when you get detached from nature, you should walk barefoot through the grass and embrace the beauty around you and within you. There is an amazing goddess inside you who drives your feminine side; it is the part of you that holds and nurtures and also creates sensitivity and mystery. Regardless of gender, it encourages optimism and insight and brings flashes of inspiration. Rainbow moonstone will support you when change is happening rapidly and steer you in the right direction if you are starting over in any way, whether in personal relationships or in your business or career.

Quartz crystal

Description: Clear or white, hexagonal prismatic crystals with pyramidal terminations and masses. May have inclusions of other crystals or minerals.
Common sources: Worldwide—commercial sources include USA (Arkansas), Brazil, China, Madagascar, Russia, Republic of South Africa, Colombia
Astrological associations: All
Chakra: All
Healing: Everything—quartz is a wonderful go-to for

crystal healers! It channels all types of energy, so, although it may not be the "best" crystal for a specific condition, it will help everything.

Crystal Connections

Keywords: Quality of life, happy, energy, focus
Crystal talk: Quartz crystal is the master crystal. First Nation peoples' traditions place him as the "Chief of the Stone People." In meditation, he brings clarity, insight, and wisdom to help you focus your mind and find the answers you need in any situation. He sheds light, which is literally focused through the crystalline structure, and brings happiness and laughter into your world. The fresh energy he gives you will chase away the blues. His message is optimistic and filled with possibilities. Quartz crystal says that you can achieve anything you set your mind to.

Lemurian quartz crystal

Description: Clear quartz hexagonal crystals with pyramidal terminations and horizontal striations—like barcodes—on their sides. Irrespective of the external appearance, internally the crystals are mostly bright and clear.
Common sources: Russia, Brazil, Colombia
Astrological associations: All
Chakra: All
Healing: Relieves pain and discomfort, helps all conditions.

Crystal Connections

Keywords: Wisdom, letting go, energy
Crystal talk: Lemurian quartz crystal links you to the ancient civilization of Lemuria and its abundant wisdom. Like all varieties of quartz, it channels any type of energy and also possesses the unique and amazing ability to translate ancient wisdom into contemporary needs, acting like an old and wise advisor. Its first message is always about your past and what you need to face, release, and

move on from. After that, it will happily go with you wherever your journey takes you. It asks you to open your heart, let go of any negativity, and share your special inner self with the world. It tells you that when you do this, you will be re-energized and refreshed, and feel happy and confident.

Apophyllite

Description: A variety from the zeolite group that forms cubic and pyramidal crystals, druses, and masses. Commonly white or colorless and, rarely, green.
Common source: India
Astrological associations: Gemini, Libra
Chakra: Brow, crown
Healing: Brain power and rejuvenation

Crystal Connections

Keywords: Meditation, connection, youthfulness
Crystal talk: Apophyllite wants you to see answers for yourself, and the best way to achieve this is through meditation. It can help you hold on to the meditative state of your mind for longer after you finish a meditation practice. This changes how you look at everything around you. Apophyllite says you should keep your eyes and all your senses open. It reminds you of youthful times when you were ready to take chances and live life to the full.

Dalmatian stone

Description: A mixture of quartz, microcline, and tourmaline, resulting in a white rock with black dots named after the Dalmatian dog breed.
Common source: Mexico
Astrological association: Gemini
Chakra: Base
Healing: Cartilage, nerves, muscles

Crystal Connections

Keywords: Calming, protecting, connecting
Crystal talk: Dalmatian stone tells you to connect with the world around you in the deepest way you can. To connect your spirit or soul to the spirits of everything around you. Whatever may be happening in your life, it reminds you to keep calm; it is only from stillness that you can see your way through whatever is worrying you. Whether it is in your home or work life, letting go of the things that trouble you from your past will free you to reach new heights.

Danburite

Description: Prismatic striated crystals that can be clear, white, pink, yellow, and lilac.
Common sources: Mexico, USA, Myanmar, Switzerland, Japan
Astrological association: Leo
Chakra: Crown
Healing: Liver, detoxing

Crystal Connections

Keywords: Socialization, go and do it
Crystal talk: Danburite carries a message of hope and a road map for you to get back into the world after an absence for any reason, such as breakdown, addiction, hospitalization, and so on. It reassures you, as you begin to meet new people and venture to new places. It will guide you to overcome the personal challenges you face along the way.

Herkimer diamond

Description: Clear, stubby, double-terminated quartz crystal
Only source: Herkimer County, New York State, USA

Astrological association: Sagittarius
Chakra: Crown
Healing: Metabolism, detoxing

Crystal Connections

Keywords: Being in the
moment, spontaneity, new
beginnings, opportunities
Crystal talk: Herkimer diamond
reminds you to be in the present moment. It talks of
openings and is always telling you to keep your eyes, and
soul, open to new possibilities. It says you need to let go
of the fears and stresses that are holding you back and
stopping you from being spontaneous. It is saying you are
holding yourself back. Release and move on is Herkimer
diamond's message.

Magnesite

Description: Masses and nodules that look a bit like
200-million-year-old chewing gum! Rarely, forms
rhombohedral, prismatic, tabular, and scalenohedral
crystals. Usually white, but may also be gray, brown, and
yellow. Can be dyed to imitate more expensive stones.
Common sources: Austria, China, USA
Astrological association: Aries
Chakra: Crown
Healing: Bones, teeth, tendons, ligaments,
cholesterol levels

Crystal Connections

Keywords: Love and passion
Crystal talk: Magnesite can be contradictory: one
moment talking about being calm and keeping things in
balance, the next telling you to let your love and passion
flow and go wherever they take you. But this is really the
same message; it is about doing the right thing at the
right time for you. It will tell you to follow the old ways
and look for new opportunities. It is all about combining
things to their best purpose and
never letting yourself be limited
by other people's
expectations.

Howlite

Description: Forms nodules, masses, and, rarely, crystals.
Often dyed to imitate more expensive stones.
Common sources: USA, Canada, Mexico, Turkey
Astrological association: Gemini
Chakra: Crown
Healing: Immune system

Crystal Connections

Keywords: Calm communication,
study, goals
Crystal talk: Howlite will calmly guide
you toward your goals. It will quietly
whisper in your ear when you get too over
the top and boisterous or fall into your own traps of
anger and selfishness. It brings you back down to that
calm place where you can communicate clearly and
express your emotions rationally. By letting go of your
ego, you let go of a lot of the stress that upsets your
otherwise calm and peaceful character.

Selenite

Description: A crystalized form of gypsum that is usually
clear or white.
Common sources: Mexico, USA, Morocco (white satin
spa variety), Canada (golden)
Astrological associations: Taurus (selenite is also linked
to the Moon—Selene is the goddess of the Moon).
Chakra: Crown
Healing: Cleansing, skin

Crystal Connections

Keywords: Cycles, fertile, timing
Crystal talk: Selenite is linked to the Moon and its cycles.
She reminds you that all of life is about cycles. Some go
round and round, just as the Moon spins around the
Earth, while others go up and down like the ocean tides
which are controlled by the Moon. And if the Moon can
move oceans, imagine what it does to your body and
mind when over 60 percent of your body is made up of
water. Selenite reminds you that success is about timing;
it is putting in the effort at exactly the right time for
maximum effect.
Often, I'm asked
to do something,
and my selenite

crystal warns me of the amount of effort required to achieve it that day. It advises me to wait, and in a few days it will tell me that it's the right time. Then whatever it is just seems to happen almost all by itself.

Snow quartz

Description: A form of quartz that occurs in white masses.
Alternate names: Quartzite, milky quartz, white quartz
Common sources: Worldwide—especially USA, India, Brazil, Mexico, France, Germany, Switzerland
Astrological association: Capricorn
Chakra: Crown
Healing: Mind

Crystal Connections

Keywords: Clarity, purity, wisdom
Crystal talk: Snow quartz can help you to clear your mind of confusing  thoughts and negativity. The negativity may be toward someone or something specific, but it affects everything you do. Snow quartz is saying that you should let it go. It is preventing you from flourishing and expressing the deep wisdom you have inside you.

Goddess stone

Description: Whitish, grayish, brownish, mineraloid opal, technically known as menalite. Forms naturally bulbous shapes, often resembling prehistoric goddess figures.
Alternate names: Menalite, fairy stone
Common sources: Morocco, Spain, USA
Astrological association: Cancer
Chakra: Crown, sacral
Healing: Fertility

Crystal Connections

Keywords: Inner goddess, sacred feminine, confidence, sensuality
Crystal talk: Goddess stone reminds you to connect with your inner goddess—we all have one, regardless of gender. It tells you about your hidden inner strengths, confidence, and powers and shows you how to connect with them, dispelling your fears and helping you discover hidden talents you were unaware of along the way. It conveys a feeling of love and nurture, supporting you in your successes and failures. Lifting you up when it needs to with kind, wise words and reminding you that there is a new beginning just around the corner, which could manifest happiness and abundance.

Tourmalinated quartz

Description: A variety of quartz with usually black tourmaline crystal rods growing through it.
Alternate name: Tourmaline in quartz
Common sources: Worldwide, but Brazil and India are the main commercial sources.
Astrological associations: All
Chakra: All
Healing: Depression, nervous system

Crystal Connections

Keywords: Problem solving, release
Crystal talk: Tourmalinated quartz suggests ways in which life could be happier and brighter for you. It lifts you up out of any state of depression by clarifying your experiences in childhood, which create the fears that stop you meeting your fullest potential. These childhood fears set up behavioral patterns that can be unhelpful and sometimes harmful later in life. It helps you work things out for yourself, guiding you along the way.

BLACK

Larvikite

Description: A black variety of feldspar, sometimes with sheen or iridescent flashes of color.
Common source: Norway
Astrological associations: Leo, Scorpio, Sagittarius
Chakra: Base, throat, brow, crown
Healing: Brings peace to emotions as they bubble to the surface.

Crystal Connections

Keywords: Relaxing, grounding, origin
Crystal talk: Larvikite teaches you how to let things come up from the seat of your soul and find expression through words or any form of creativity, music, or art. Place a piece under your pillow and it will speak to you in your dreams.

Jet

Description: A type of lignite formed from fossilized trees.
Common sources: Worldwide—especially UK (Whitby), Canada, France, Spain, USA
Astrological association: Capricorn
Chakra: Base
Healing: Migraine, common cold, stomach ache

Crystal Connections

Keywords: Calm, energy, grounding
Crystal talk: When life gets tough, jet is a crystal friend to have by your side. Talking you out of depression and giving you the strength to face your fears, it calms and energizes at the same time. It says that you should keep a foot on the ground as you take each idea one step at a time.

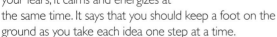

Obsidian

Description: Natural volcanic glass that occurs in a variety of colors, including black, brown, green, red/black, brown/black, mahogany, black with rainbow colors, silver or gold sheen, black with white snowflake patterns, blue, purple, translucent black and brown nodules.
Common sources: Worldwide—especially Mexico, USA, Iceland, Italy, Japan, Peru, Russia
Astrological associations: Scorpio, Sagittarius, Capricorn
Chakra: Base
Healing: Digestion, male sexuality

Crystal Connections

Keywords: Wisdom, protection, creativity, recognizing the cause of dis-ease
Crystal talk: Obsidian will point out your self-defeating patterns and subconscious blockages, so you can bring them to the surface and change what you are doing. It acts as a mirror for your soul, so you can understand what's happening deep inside you. It reflects without judgment, so you see your best and worst characteristics, leading to the possibility of long-lasting positive change.

Melanite

Description: A black variety of garnet that forms dodecahedral crystals and masses.
Common sources: Brazil, USA, Italy, Australia, Canada, China, Germany, India, Japan, Kazakhstan, Kenya
Astrological association: Scorpio
Chakra: Heart
Healing: Stroke, arthritis, side effects of medication

Crystal Connections

Keywords: Trust, calmness
Crystal talk: A perfect crystal for any situation in which trust is required. It reminds you that your suspicions breed more suspicion. So, change your viewpoint and trust

everything that you can to encourage more trust. It is a helpful ally in confrontations, helping you to find a peaceful resolution.

Black tourmaline

Description: Black, vertically striated prismatic crystals
Alternate name: Schorl
Common sources: Brazil, India, Pakistan, Kenya, Mozambique, Namibia, Zambia
Astrological association: Capricorn
Chakra: Base
Healing: Heart, adrenal glands, arthritis

Crystal Connections

Keywords: Protection, creativity, intellect, grounding
Crystal talk: Black tourmaline tells you that you are okay. It gives you confidence and reassures you that it is looking after you and will keep any negative vibes away. This helps you to let go of any anxiety or embarrassment and to express the real you to the world, while all the time reminding you to keep your feet firmly on the ground.

Merlinite

Description: Black and white moss opal
Common sources: Turkey, India, USA
Astrological association: Pisces
Chakra: Brow
Healing: Reproduction

Crystal Connections

Keywords: Mystery, magical
Crystal talk: When there is disagreement merlinite tells you to look at things from the other's point of view. It is bubbling with optimism and its advice will ease your way forward in life. Opportunities seem to arise magically and merlinite tells you to grasp these and move forward as your life begins to flow.

Goethite

Description: Forms scales, fibers, prismatic crystals, needle-like structures, masses, radial stalactites, and "pipe organ" structures. Colors include black, brown, yellow, orange and red.
Common sources: Brazil, Madagascar, Morocco, France, USA, Republic of South Africa, Russia, Australia
Astrological association: Aries
Chakra: Brow
Healing: Ears, nose, and throat, digestion, blood loss

Crystal Connections

Keywords: Fun, living life to the full
Crystal talk: Goethite says, "If you're not having fun, you're doing something wrong!" And it helps you to enjoy life while keeping you safe. It translates the energy of spirit guides into words you can understand, so you can follow their guidance as you step out and live life to the full.

GRAY AND SILVER CRYSTALS

Gray banded agate

Description: A variety of chalcedony with gray and white banding.
Common source: Botswana
Astrological association: Scorpio
Chakra: Sacral
Healing: Energy, fatigue, general malaise

Crystal Connections

Keywords: Protection, emotional security
Crystal talk: Gray banded agate wants to wrap its arms around you to comfort you and make you feel safe. It advises you to stop worrying about what other people think and move on. It is always looking out for you and warning of any danger or negativity coming your way.

Pyrite

Description: Cubic and dodecahedral crystals, occasionally flattened (pyrite suns) and masses. Becomes more golden with oxidation and may replace many minerals, so can be found in other shapes and formations and in combination with other minerals.
Common sources: Worldwide—especially Italy, China, Peru, Spain, USA, UK, Kazakhstan, Netherlands, Russia
Astrological association: Leo
Chakra: Solar plexus, all
Healing: Circulation, bones, lungs

Crystal Connections

Keywords: Inspiration, memories, energy
Crystal talk: Pyrite brings sparks of inspiration. Its wisdom often seems too simple, but it is the many simple pieces that complete a complex puzzle. It also gives your memory hints to help you avoid repeating errors and to find your winning ways.

Hematite

Description: Commonly polished to a metallic silver/gray, but naturally occurs as masses, botryoidal forms, rosettes, layered plates, and tabular and rhombohedral crystals. May be black or brick red/brown as well as metallic silver/gray.
Common sources: Worldwide—especially UK, Morocco, USA, Brazil, Canada
Astrological associations: Aries, Aquarius
Chakra: Base
Healing: Blood, travel sickness, jet lag

Crystal Connections

Keywords: Grounding, going the extra mile, personal magnetism
Crystal talk: Hematite keeps your feet on the ground. It whispers words of encouragement when you feel you have given your all—you will discover that you have a little bit more to give. This determination draws others toward you, so you find you have the allies you need around you.

Stibnite

Description: Needle-like and prismatic crystals, masses, columns, and blades
Common sources: Uzbekistan, China, Japan, USA
Astrological associations: Scorpio, Capricorn
Chakra: Crown
Healing: Learning lessons from illness or other problems

Crystal Connections

Keywords: Decisions, teaching, learning, animal guides
Crystal talk: Stibnite connects to the wolf, which is considered a teacher in many traditions. It guides you toward the knowledge you need in the moment to help you deal or cope with any situation. It will give you the words you need in tricky situations, such as releasing you from relationships or business partnerships when it is time to move on.

BROWN

Aragonite

Description: Hexagonal, column-shaped crystals that are often interlocked to form "sputnik" shapes. Also, fibers, masses, and stalactites. Colors include brown, white, yellow, blue, and green.
Common sources: Morocco, Namibia, Austria, Germany, Italy, Greece, Spain, Japan, China
Astrological association: Capricorn
Chakra: Crown
Healing: Skin, especially stress-related skin conditions

Crystal Connections

Keywords: Answers, patience, practicality, reliability
Crystal talk: Aragonite has the knack of making answers suddenly appear, as if from out of thin air. However, it also reminds you to be patient and wait for the right moment before making your move. In the

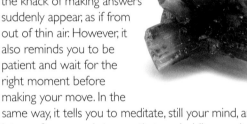

same way, it tells you to meditate, still your mind, and let go of anger and stresses that are holding you back. You can be your own worst enemy.

Crazy lace agate

Description: A variety of chalcedony with "crazy" patterns and bands of cream, red, and brown
Alternate name: Mexican lace agate
Common source: Mexico
Astrological associations: Gemini, Capricorn, Aquarius
Chakra: Heart
Healing: Heart, physical senses

Crystal Connections

Keywords: Confidence, courage, self-esteem
Crystal talk: Crazy lace agate speaks the words you need to hear to dispel any fears you may have. Then it holds your hand and inspires confidence as you move forward. In fact, it is my go-to crystal for confidence for anyone, of any age, and for any reason! It brings that courage, inner strength, and self-esteem you sometimes need.

Petrified wood

Description: Fossilized trees in which the organic material has been replaced by one or more minerals—usually agate, chalcedony, or quartz (but others may also be present). The word petrified literally means "turned to stone." Colors include brown, but can be any wood-like color or the natural colors of agate, chalcedony, and sometimes opal.
Common sources: Worldwide—especially USA, Madagascar, Australia
Astrological association: Leo
Chakra: Base
Healing: Stress, bones, arthritis

Crystal Connections

Keywords: The past, childhood, past lives
Crystal talk: Petrified wood tells you to stay the course and stick to your guns. You are worth the effort. It also explains how some of your stresses are linked to past experiences, especially from childhood and possibly further back into your past lives. Recognizing this can help you to let go of the cause and therefore the stress you are currently experiencing.

Smoky quartz

Description: A brown or black variety of quartz colored by natural radiation from the Earth. This process can be effectively duplicated in laboratories and some smoky quartz on the market is thus man-made or enhanced.
Common sources: Brazil, Madagascar, USA, Mozambique
Astrological associations: Sagittarius, Capricorn

Chakra: Base
Healing: Grief

Crystal Connections

Keywords: Inner god, moving forward in life
Crystal talk: Smoky quartz is a powerful friend to have in your corner. It helps you tune in to your inner god—which we all have, regardless of gender—and listen to his advice. It also speaks soothing words when you suffer a loss or are grieving. It will guide you on your journey, step by step, as you move forward and protect you from the negativity, ill thoughts, and intentions of others.

Septarian

Description: Nodules of clay ironstone into which calcite, jasper, dolomite, aragonite, and, occasionally, barite, are deposited through small cracks in the structure.
Common sources: Australia, Madagascar, USA
Astrological association: Taurus
Chakra: Base
Healing: Flexibility, bones, muscles, joints

Crystal Connections

Keywords: Patience, tolerance, endurance
Crystal talk: Septarian is the quiet advisor, suggesting emotional flexibility. It roots for patience and tolerance rather than impulsiveness and conflict. It always recommends taking the long view of any situation, even if that results in short-term loss for long-term gain.

Muscovite

Description: A variety of mica-forming "plates," "flowers," "books," scales, masses, and other crystalline forms. Colors include brown, green, pink, gray, violet, yellow, red, and white.
Common sources: Brazil, India, Pakistan, USA
Astrological associations: Leo, Aquarius
Chakra: Heart

Healing: Letting go of the image you created for yourself, whether consciously or not.

Crystal Connections

Keywords: Emotional expression, confidence, assuredness
Crystal talk: Muscovite will cut through your ego and reflect the true you to yourself. When you see this, you can let go of the image that you created around yourself as a form of protection from painful memories. In doing this, you can release your newly found, confident, optimistic, and happy inner self into the world.

Rutile/rutilated quartz

Description: Needle-like crystals, often penetrating quartz (rutilated quartz), and prismatic crystals. Colors include bronze, silver, red, brown, red/brown, black, yellow, gold, and violet.
Common sources: Brazil, Australia, Ukraine, Norway, Pakistan, Kazakhstan, Republic of South Africa
Astrological associations: Taurus, Gemini
Chakra: Brow
Healing: Tackles the cause of dis-ease, aura

Crystal Connections

Keywords: Mental balance, remote viewing
Crystal talk: Rutile opens horizons for you, both physically with opportunities and, psychically, by being aware of distant places (rutilated quartz works just as well). It calls on you to act on this information and reassures you that just like its resemblance to angel hair, your guardians are always with you.

Crystal Index

Page numbers in bold refer to entries in the Crystal Finder

agate 21
  blue lace **123**
  crazy lace **138**
  fire **120**
  gray banded **137**
  pink banded **117–18**
alexandrite 29, 54
amazonite **113–14**
amber **110**
amethyst 20, 22, 25, 42, 44, 83, **128**
  banded **130**
  black 27
angel aura quartz **122**
angelite **124**
apophyllite **132**
aqua aura 70, **126**
aquamarine **124**
aragonite **138**
aventurine **112**

banded amethyst **130**
black amethyst 27
black tourmaline schorl **136**
blue apatite **123**
blue calcite 21, **125**
blue chalcedony **123**
blue lace agate **123**
blue tourmaline/indicolite **127**
bowenite **114–15**
brecciated jasper 21, **105**

calcite 20, 27
  blue 21, **125**
  cobaltoan **118–19**
  golden **109**
  green 27, **114**
  orange 21, 27, 78, **107**
  red **106**
carnelian 42, 78, 92, **107**
catlinite (pipestone) 13
celestite 17, 40, 43, **125**
chalcedony 107, 115, 137, 138
  blue **123**
chalcopyrite 43, **120–21**
chrysoberyl 29
chrysocolla **113**
chrysoprase **115**
citrine 20, 22–23, 25, 35, 80, **109**
cobaltoan calcite **118–19**
copper 40, **110**
crazy lace agate **138**

Dalmatian stone **132**
danburite **132**

emerald **114**

fire agate **120**
fluorite
  purple **129**
  rainbow **121**
  yellow **111**

garnet **106**
goddess stone **134**
goethite **136**
golden calcite **109**
golden healer quartz **108–109**
gray banded agate **137**
green calcite 27, **114**
green tourmaline **116**

halite (rock salt) 20, 43
hematite 78, **137**
Herkhimer diamond **132–33**
howlite **133**

imperial topaz **110–11**

jade **112**
jasper
  brecciated 21, **105**
  red 78, **105**
jet **135**

kunzite **117**
kyanite 82, **123–24**

labradorite 83, **120**
lapis lazuli 20, 25, 82, **125**
larvikite **135**
Lemurian quartz 16, **131–32**
lepidolite **128**

magnesite 133
malachite 21, 40, 69, 81, 112–13
melanite 135–36
merlinite 136
moldavite 116
morganite 119
muscovite 139

obsidian 135
opal 121
  pink 117
orange calcite 21, 27, 78, 107

peridot 115
petrified wood 138
pink banded agate 117–18
pink opal 117
pink tourmaline 119
purple fluorite 129
pyrite 20, 68, 137

quartz 11, 12, 14, 16, 21, 29, 31, 36–38, 42, 44, 54, 98, 100
  angel aura 122
  golden healer 108–109
  Lemurian quartz crystal 16, 36–37, 131–32
  quartz crystal 131
  rose 20, 27, 65, 68, 117
  rutile/rutilated 139
  smoky 138–39
  snow 134
  spirit 130
  strawberry 119
  titanium 122
  tourmalinated 134

rainbow fluorite 121
rainbow moonstone 131
red calcite 106
red jasper 78, 105
rhodochrosite 21, 118
rhodonite 118
rose quartz 20, 27, 65, 68, 117
ruby 14, 54, 81, 105
rutile/rutilated quartz 139

sapphire 54, 126
selenite 11, 17, 20, 40, 42, 43, 69, 133–34
septarian 139
smoky quartz 138–39
snow quartz 134
spirit quartz 130
stibnite 137
strawberry quartz 119
sugilite 21, 129–30
sunstone 108
super seven 129

tanzanite 29, 82, 126–27
tektite 116
tiger's eye 111
titanium quartz 122
tourmalinated quartz 134

tourmaline 14, 20, 21, 29, 54
  black tourmaline schorl 136
  blue 127
  green 116
  pink 119
  watermelon 122
turquoise 82, 127

unakite 113

vortex healing crystal 40, 43, 107

watermelon tourmaline 122

yellow fluorite 111

zircon 106

General Index

African divination baskets 93
amethyst beds 27, 42
amethyst geodes 27, 42
art projects, crystals and 68
astragali 92
auras 74–76
  astral aura 76
  emotional aura 75–76
  etheric aura 75
  feeling and sensing crystals
    with your aura 87
  higher mental plane aura 76
  lower mental plane aura 76
  physical aura 75
  vital aura 75, 76

bacteria and viruses 10
bathing elixirs 65
black crystals 28, 135–36
blue crystals 28, 123–27
bodymind 74
  see also human energy system
brown crystals 28, 138–39
burying crystals in the
    ground 42
buying crystals 55, 57–58, 59
  for someone else 59
buying pendulums 25–26

calming effect 21
carrying crystals with you 63
chakras 74, 77–83
  aids for diagnosis 87
  balancing 89
  base chakra 77, 78

brow chakra (third eye chakra)
    77, 82
  connecting with your chakras
    88–89
  crown chakra 77, 83
  feeling and sensing crystals
    with your chakras 86
  heart chakra 77, 81
  laying on of stones 100–101
  meditation 88–89
  sacral chakra 77, 78
  solar plexus chakra 77, 80
  throat chakra 77, 82
charging crystals 61
chi (qi) 79
choosing crystals 22, 44–45,
    47–49
  meditation 50–51
  special qualities 47
  using your senses 48–49
cleansing crystals 17, 39–43,
    57–59
  with the breath 42
  new crystals 57–59
  rebirth ritual (burying your
    crystal) 42
  salt, avoiding 43
  smudging 41
  sound cleansing 40
  under a full moon 41
  washing 40
  when it is needed 39
  working with other crystals 42
clear and white crystals 28,
    131–34

colors 27–30
  changing color 27, 29
  and influences 28–29
  sensing crystal colors 30
  see also specific colors
communicating with crystals 31,
    34–35, 45, 46, 57
  opening your heart 46
Cradle of Humankind 14–15, 92
crystal balls 92
crystal casting 97
crystal energy 14–17, 19, 43,
    61, 69
  sensing 16–17
crystal grids 98–99
crystal technology 14, 15, 54
crystals
  age 11, 44
  buying 55, 57–58, 59
  cleansing 17, 39–43, 57–59
  colors 27–30
  communicating with 31, 34–35,
    45, 46, 57
  connecting with 23–26, 70–71
  crystal finder 102–39
  crystal hunting 55–57, 58–59
  first life forms 13
  friendships with 19, 34–35
  growth 11
  how crystals can help 20–21
  intelligence 12
  listening to 19, 31, 45, 57
  as living beings 10–13, 19, 34
  in nature 55–56, 58–59
  reproduction 11, 12

selecting 22, 44–45, 47–49
working with 63–69

dark matter and dark energy
    64, 79
dedicating crystals 62
divination 90–101
    crystal casting 97
    crystal grids 98–99
    crystal reading 96, 100
    divination baskets 93, 94–95
    history of 92–93
    laying on of stones 100–101
    meditations 101
    what it is 92
dowsing 23

early humans
    crystals and 15
    divination and 92
elixirs 68–69
    drinking 68, 69
    topical 68
energy
    chi (qi) 79
    dark energy 64, 79
    kundalini 78
    negative energy 20, 39, 61
    see also crystal energy; human
        energy system

First Nation peoples 41
fossils 15, 44
free will 44

gray and silver crystals 29, 137
Greeks, ancient 92–93
green crystals 29, 112–16

healing 21, 62
    placing crystals on the body
        66–67
    quartz master crystals 36–37,
        62
Hippocrates 93
Homer 92
human energy system 72–89
    auras see auras
    chakras see chakras
    energy exercises 84–89
    energy hot spots 74, 77, 81, 83,
        85
    meridians see meridians
    Universal Life Force Energy 79
humors, theory of the 93

indigo crystals 28
indoor plants, healthy 21
inspiration 20

jewelry, wearing crystals as 63
Judeo-Christian Bible 92

Ki 79
kundalini 78

listening to crystals 19, 31, 45,
    57
loving relationships 21

meditations
    choosing crystals 50–51
    connecting with your chakras
        88–89
    connecting with your crystal's
        spirit 70–71
    crystal divination meditation
        101
    listening to your crystals 31
    meditation preparation 18
    sensing crystal energy 16–17
meridians 74, 77, 83

nadis see meridians
negativity, transforming 20
new crystals
    charging 61
    cleansing 57–59
    dedicating 62
    programming 62
    welcoming into your home
        60–62

online purchases
    crystals 55, 59
    pendulums 26
orange crystals 28, 107–108
pendulum 23–26
    choosing and buying 25–26
    crystal pendulum 23, 24–26,
        59
    inner pendulum 24, 34, 80
    working with 24
pink crystals 28, 117–19
pleochroism 29

prana 79
programming crystals 62
protection 20

quartz crystal beds 42
quartz master crystals 36–37, 62
  choosing 38

rainbow and multicolored
  crystals 28, 120–22
red crystals 28, 105–106
relaxation 20
resting your crystals 27, 42

scrying 92
seeding reproduction method
  11, 12
sensitivity 20
Sibyls 92
smudging 41
Socrates 92, 93

tingsha 40
touch effect 63
tranquillity 20

violet crystals 29, 128–30

water divining 23
white crystals see clear and
  white crystals
working with crystals 63–69
  in art 68
  carrying crystals 63
  changing crystals 65
  elixirs 68–69
  keeping crystals around you
  65
  placing crystals on the body
  66–67
worries, easing 21

yellow crystals 28

Acknowledgments

I would like to thank my staff at The Crystal Healer, Steph, Claire, Steph Steph, Heather, and Rachel who are now affectionately known as the Crystal Healer Helpers. Without them it would be difficult to find the time to write this book. All my clients, students, customers, and friends who inspire me to go further and discover more about the world of the Stone People every day and provide a wealth of experience for me to share with you. The people at CICO Books; especially Carmel Edmonds who helped to get this book off the ground and Slav Todorov for his patience!!

Thank you, Cindy Richards, for having faith in the beginning.

A fabulously big thank you to my fabulous partner Nicci for pushing me to the highest levels! And for lovingly being here.

Finally, the people who inspired me to write: my father Cyril and American crystal healer Melody, and Ian, who knows why.

Picture credits

ADOBE STOCK
26454562 (Mist) 2, 8, 32, 52, 72, 90, 102; 259716760 (MarinaErmakova) 1, 2, 3, 8, 9, 32, 33, 38, 46, 48, 49, 50, 52, 53, 66, 67, 70, 71, 72, 73, 84, 85, 86, 88, 89, 90, 91, 94, 95, 96, 98, 99, 100, 102, 103; 379355862 (alkini) p. 10, 11, 14 (top), 15, 19 (top), 22 (top), 23 (top), 35 (top), 36, 37, 40 (bottom), 42, 51, 54 (top), 55 (top), 57, 59 (top), 60, 64, 68 (top), 69 (top), 76, 83, 96 (top), 97 (top); 332450402 (Damian) 10 (bottom); 333090694 (Creative Wonder) 10 (middle); 128549555 (Paulista) 10 (top); 326420665 (Phibonacci) 13 (top right); 509086421 (Tetiana) 13 (top middle); 25007246 (Mike Richter) 14 (top); 94873859 (spiritofamerica) 14 (bottom); 324304183 (Giovanni Cancemi) 15; 299656591 (New Africa) 19 (bottom); 348145889 (fad82) 36; 487000036 (Katelin) 51; 518042147 (evannovostro) 54; 317334537 (Oleksandr) 58 (bottom); 510680439 (Elena) 59 (top); 336697522 (sakkmesterke) 64; 192790378 (tomertu) 68 (bottom);

86666865 (Nikki Zalewski) 79 (top); 307738199 (yurchello108) 83 (bottom); 59709658 (viktoriya89) 92; 463883321 (ellenbessonova) 96 (top); 237256589 (tomatito26) 122 (bottom left)

SHUTTERSTOCK
1270819777 (Nadiinko) 9 (bottom), 26, 32 (bottom), 44 (top), 51 (bottom), 53 (bottom), 60 (bottom), 71 (top), 73 (bottom), 91 (bottom), 103 (bottom)